THE ART OF CLOSING

THE ART OF CLOSING

ANYONE, ANYWHERE, ANYTIME

ZED NASHEET

First published in 2026 by Dean Publishing
PO Box 119
Mt. Macedon, Victoria, 3441
Australia
deanpublishing.com

DEAN PUBLISHING

Cataloguing-in-Publication Data
National Library of Australia

Title: The Art of Closing Anyone, Anywhere, Anytime
ISBN: 978-1-764561-91-4
Category: Business/Sales

CONTENTS

ABOUT ZED....1

INTRODUCTION....3

ZELLING....11

A CAREER IN REAL ESTATE....45

NEGOTIATION....95

BRANDING....117

MARKETING....133

YOU, YOUR MINDSET AND SUCCESS....169

BUILDING CONNECTIONS....249

ZOLD!....277

ACKNOWLEDGEMENTS....281

ENDNOTES....283

ABOUT ZED

Zed Nasheet didn't just rise to the top – he exploded onto the stage of Australian real estate.

In 2021, he became Victoria's Number One Agent after transacting an extraordinary $209 million in property, selling over 120 homes at an average price of $2.2 million. Today, Zed moves in an entirely different league, with an average sale price above $5 million, representing some of the most prestigious homes and elite clients in the country.

A magnetic force in the industry, Zed is often described as a new-generation real estate phenomenon – a blend of Hollywood charisma, entrepreneurial genius, and relentless, unstoppable ambition. His screen presence and unique marketing style have seen him featured across major Australian TV networks, global media streams, and even Netflix.

Drawing inspiration from his roots, Zed has become an icon for millions across Afghanistan and beyond. His online courses, mentorship programs, and global subscriber community follow not just an agent – but a movement. As the founder of one of Australia's most-followed real estate agencies, Zed reshapes the luxury experience with cinematic marketing, bold storytelling, and electric energy.

In 2021, he broke an industry milestone by selling over $60 million worth of real estate in a single month – an achievement that shook the industry and cemented his status as a trailblazer. Long before the industry caught up, Zed pioneered high-end cinematic advertising and social media campaigns that revolutionised the way luxury properties are marketed.

Driven by a work ethic that rivals an Olympian, Zed Nasheet has become synonymous with luxury, mastery, and market domination. His foundation is built on unwavering ethics, strong family values, and advanced mastery in human behaviour and high-stakes negotiation.

Zed Nasheet is not just a real estate agent – he is a global brand, a visionary leader, and the future of luxury real estate.

zedrealestate.au

INTRODUCTION

If you're someone who is ready to break free from mediocrity, to take control of your future, and to push past the limits you've set for yourself, then keep reading. This book is for those who are ready to fight for their dreams, who believe that true success is earned.

BUILT ON HUNGER: CONFIDENCE, RISK, AND SUCCESS

I was 12 years old when my family came to Australia, and we arrived with a dream and a purpose – to have a comfortable life and better opportunities, without the fear that comes from living in a war-torn country: being kidnapped, having to pay ransom, or worse.

Afghanistan had been a war zone for as long as I can remember, in fact even before my birth. My family didn't come here to settle for average. Dad had everything before the war and lost it all because of it. He always taught us that there is no such thing as a big job or a small job, as long as it's earned the right way, and you go to sleep with peace in your mind. That's why I say Australia is the land of opportunity – it's where dreams are made, and where you can make it big. If you can dream it, you can achieve it. I'm so grateful and lucky to call Melbourne home, away from the war, away from all the daily troubles we faced back home.

A lot of people take this country for granted. They have it too easy; they're comfortable, and most people are caught up in much smaller problems than what we went through. The best thing that happened to me was experiencing poverty. That's where my drive, energy, motivation, and confidence come from – my background and the experiences I had in my childhood.

I remember the day we were in our lounge when I was nine years old. My older brother, Qaiss, was feeding me and my other brother, Tawab, a bowl of rice. Meat was very expensive; only the rich could afford it. We couldn't even afford soft drinks. Qaiss's exact words were, "I'll put bread in the bowl, and you guys pretend it's chicken." We used to shower in the courtyard in front of others, using a bucket and bowl to pour water over ourselves. It took two people to wash – one to pour the water and one to scrub. I saw proper bathrooms and toilets for the first time when we came to Australia.

If it weren't for my hunger, and confidence, I wouldn't be where I am today. Hunger led me to action, and action is the key to success. A tough person gets the job done, and my clients could feel how hungry I was to get the job done.

I would use my hunger as part of my selling pitch: my competitors are already big – they won't work as hard as I will while I'm trying to make a name for myself. I would love to represent you in the marketplace, not to treat you like a number, but to achieve the best results and service for the biggest asset of your life. This pitch always helped me connect with clients.

Self-confidence is believing in yourself – your own skills, abilities, and talents. People are drawn to confidence, and they prefer to deal with those who carry it well.

But you also must make sure you're not *too* confident, or people might see you as cocky or full of yourself. There's a big difference between being arrogant and being confident. Confidence is knowing your place in life and embracing who you are in an honest, grounded way. Arrogance is thinking you're better than everyone else. As a salesman, you must be confident. Confidence is what brings deals together. If it weren't for my self-belief, I wouldn't have sold some of the most expensive real estate in the country – and Z. Real Estate wouldn't exist today.

It was that same self-confidence that led me to create the word **ZOLD**. I knew it would stand out in the marketplace, and that I'd become known as **Mr. ZOLD**. I believed in it – and that belief helped me achieve what I set out to do: disrupt the marketplace.

It's my confidence that stands out in my marketplace. If I want something, I go after it. I don't doubt myself or my ability for a single minute. If I'm unsure about something, I find out more information before making a decision. If I make a mistake, I learn from it.

It's not just about taking risks. People take risks all the time, but they have too many advisers and don't listen to their gut feeling or inner voice. Too many people put negativity in your brain, and it prevents you from doing what you want to do. Imagine how many people told Steve Ditko, the American comic artist, that nobody would like Spider-Man. Imagine if he hadn't taken that risk. Superheroes like Batman, Superman, and Spider-Man wouldn't be a part of our culture.

"

IN BUSINESS, IT'S NOT ABOUT WHO YOU KNOW; IT'S ABOUT WHO KNOWS YOU. IT'S ABOUT TAKING CALCULATED RISKS AND TRUSTING YOUR GUT FEELING.

"

FROM HUMBLE BEGINNINGS TO ENDLESS OPPORTUNITIES

After only two years in Australia, I launched my sales career. I was 14 and set up a hot dog stand outside nightclubs in Melbourne, three nights each weekend from 9:00 pm to 6:00 am. The hot dogs were supposed to sell for $4, but I sold them for $80. I was young, of course, but I learnt how to negotiate, how to soft-sell and how to build rapport with your customer.

When I first got into real estate, I was 21 and broke, driving my old Holden Barina. I bought it at a car auction for $1,200, and it was the best thing that happened to me back then. It was a wise investment for me – reliable, economical, and $10 of fuel would last me three days. But I would always park it 500 metres away from a potential client's home. The last thing I wanted was for them to see what type of car I drove; even knowing this was the beginning of my journey.

My biggest motivation was my mum and dad. They have done everything for my three brothers and me to make sure we have a good education and live a comfortable lifestyle. Whether Dad was washing dishes at a restaurant, cleaning, or working in retail, he always told us there's no such thing as a big or small job – as long as it's done with integrity and honesty.

This is where my motivation comes from: to work hard and give my parents the comfort they gave us when we were growing up. I had no mentor when I started, and it was a big deal for me to walk into someone's house and discuss their biggest asset.

You are dealing with people's livelihood – a place where their kids are raised, where they have memories with their loved ones, and where they work their whole life to pay off a 30-year mortgage. The moral of the story is: Don't be afraid to step outside your comfort zone and take risks you weren't expecting to take. Always remember that it's not the size of the opportunity that matters. Small opportunities often lead to bigger opportunities in the future. So, be open and take advantage when the opportunity arrives.

CONSISTENCY CREATES OPPORTUNITY

There are 86,400 seconds in a day and 1,440 minutes. Every second and every minute counts because we can't buy time. I thank God every day for another chance to bring positive energy to the world. Having a positive mindset plays a big role in sales, as you're always facing challenges and people's problems. It's our job to build a strong positive relationship with people so they can refer you to their friends and families. The best advertising is word-of-mouth. But at the start of your career, focus on building relationships, regardless of where you are.

The two work hand in hand.

> "
>
> **IF YOU CAN MAKE A LITTLE PROGRESS EVERY SINGLE DAY AND HAVE THE PATIENCE TO WAIT FOR THAT TO ACCUMULATE, YOU WILL BE ABLE TO REACH EVEN THE HIGHEST GOALS.**
>
> "

Real estate is a long-term game, so be prepared for it. Property prices in Australia double every 7 to 10 years. Set big success goals then draft a roadmap that will lead to your goal. Work on some milestones along the way to mark your progress.

With that done, your next step is to determine what you need. This quote from Jim Rohn has changed my life: 'What you lack in skill, you make up for in numbers'. The more people you talk to, the more opportunities you create for your business. You will have more chances of succeeding in your business rather than waiting for hope or waiting for that phone to ring. Success doesn't happen overnight; it takes hard work and time. That's why some of the best basic success skills you can develop are patience and persistence. I highly recommend the movie *The Founder*, about how McDonald's was developed. In the movie, Ray Kroc says, 'It was my persistence and hard work that got me to where I am'.

Milestones help you realise and celebrate your progress. Think of them as frequent reminders that persistence pays off and that it requires patience to reach those really big goals.

This kind of persistence and discipline doesn't come easily to most people. It takes effort, hard work, and it requires you to build habits that reinforce these skills on a daily basis.

Even if things don't work out, whatever you do, don't give up. Keep practising discipline and persistence, and they'll quickly become habits that are part of who you are and how you work.

PROTECT YOUR ENERGY, PROTECT YOUR BUSINESS

In business – and especially in real estate – your **energy is just as valuable as your bank account**. The way you spend it will determine the kind of business you attract, the quality of relationships you build, and ultimately, the level of success you reach.

Just like you wouldn't throw money at a bad investment, you shouldn't pour energy into people or deals that don't align with your values.

Start treating your energy as a limited resource, because it is. Make sure you choose clients who respect your process. Choose appointments that excite you, not drain you. And choose deals that are a genuine win for all parties – not just a pay cheque.

"

IF SOMETHING FEELS OFF, THERE'S A REASON. YOUR GUT IS A SMARTER BUSINESS TOOL THAN MOST PEOPLE GIVE IT CREDIT FOR. LEARN TO TRUST IT.

"

TEACH PEOPLE HOW TO TREAT YOU

If you consistently allow clients to disrespect your boundaries, waste your time, or question your value – you're teaching the world how to treat you.

Setting boundaries isn't arrogant. It's leadership.

Teach people how to treat you by operating from a place of confidence, alignment, and self-respect. The right clients will be drawn to that.

ZELLING

Becoming great at selling does not happen immediately. You get great at selling day by day. The best salespeople are the ones with the best attitude, the best product knowledge, and the best service.

Sales is not simply a matter of leads, appointments, and closes. It is not even just a matter of the quality of your product or the speed of your service. Sales is a matter of who you are, what your attitude is, and how dedicated you are to personal excellence. It is about how responsible you are for the actions you take and how sincere you are about helping others win for themselves so that, ultimately, you can win for yourself. That is not just an idea or a strategy. That is a philosophy.

But the biggest non-secret that salespeople fail to embrace is consistent daily action towards achievement.

1. **The Value of Establishing a Friendly Relationship.** All things being equal, people want to do business with their friends. All things being not quite so equal, people still want to do business with their friends.
2. **The Value of Humour.** If you can make them laugh, you can make them buy. Study humour.
3. **The Value of Believing in Yourself.** To make a sale, you have to believe you work for the greatest company in the world. Z. Real Estate is by far the greatest agency and organisation in the universe. Customers do not pay you for what you do; they pay you for why you do it. People always buy you first and then the brand. The brand is only as good as your pitch. You have to believe you have the greatest products and services in the world. You have to believe you are the

greatest person in the world. Four key words: you have to believe.

4. **The Value of Being Prepared.** Most salespeople are half-prepared. They know everything about themselves, but they know nothing about their prospects. Study the client. Find out what field they are in, and even their hobbies. Look at their social media and learn about their interests and how many kids they have, so they know you have done your research and appreciate it. Become their friend by asking questions. People buy from friends more often. Do not forget to be yourself. The more you talk about them and ask about them, the more they will like you.

Before you begin, ask yourself the following questions:

- How well do I think I sell?
- How do I practise my skills every day?
- How much time do I spend learning new sales skills?
- How many new ideas do I put into practice daily?
- How dedicated and committed to success am I?

Sales is a discipline. Not a militaristic kind of discipline, like 'do it or peel potatoes', but a personal dedication to achievement that can only occur when discipline is present. It is control that comes from within, not rules imposed from without. Not the drudgery of discipline, but the joy of it.

Discipline is the everyday process of focusing on what you want and striving for it relentlessly until you get it.

NINE TIPS FOR BECOMING THE BEST REAL ESTATE AGENT

There are many good reasons to become a real estate agent. You're running a business within a business. You have leaders to look up to and be inspired by on a daily basis. It's up to you how much money you want to make – profit-driven businesses are better than earning a wage. The flexibility is also a huge advantage: you can make your own hours, earn good money, and help people find their dream homes. And if you're going to put in all that hard work and effort to become a real estate agent, you might as well strive to be the best one. Whether you're new to the business or experienced, there's always room for improvement.

1. Learn the Art of Communication

Communication is key in all areas of life. In real estate, it's imperative. I'm always available for my clients, no matter the day, and I never tell them I'm too busy to answer their calls. People don't sell their biggest assets every day, so your job as an agent is to over-service them, communicate with them daily, and take the pressure off their shoulders. People buy from those they like and trust, so learn how to sell by genuinely being there for your clients and listening to them.

2. Form Partnerships

If you want to succeed in any business, you need to know that you can't do it all on your own. You need continuous support from business partners who share the same work ethic. Form partnerships with professionals like bankers, builders, interior designers, and even gardeners. These partnerships will provide valuable referrals, and you can return the favour.

3. Pitch Stories to Reporters and PR

Reporters are always looking for fresh story angles. I get a lot of press and editorials on my properties and brand because of existing relationships. It's not hard to build a relationship with journalists – simply pick up the phone, dial, and introduce yourself. That's their job; they want news and interesting stories. Stay in touch with journalists, share your good news, and become their go-to source for real estate stories.

4. Open Houses

Open houses are a great way to meet the local community and build your database. Neighbours are always curious about how much a property is listed for or what it sold for. It's a great way to generate new leads and offer clients a real feel for a property. Even though technology allows clients to view homes online, nothing beats seeing a property in person. Open houses give you the chance to show what you can sell and connect with fresh faces.

5. Have an Online Presence

When you create a website, you want people to visit and browse it, but with social media, you don't need to wait for them to come to you. They're available at your fingertips – essentially, it's your personal website. Nearly everyone is online, and if you're not, you'll never become the best real estate agent. Every time I make a new connection, I follow or add them on at least one of my social channels.

6. Maintain Relationships

If you're new to the game, staying in touch with your clients – even after you've helped them buy their dream home – is crucial. There's no point in working on cold leads when you have existing relationships. Call your clients every six months and stay in touch. They're more likely to recommend you to friends and family.

7. Qualify Your Clients

When I get an enquiry on a property I've just launched, I don't just take them through. I ask three questions to help me find out their motivation and focus on serious buyers:

- Have you organised your finances?
- Do you have a pre-approval?
- Are you ready to purchase today if I show you the property?

If they've just started browsing, I'll recommend they attend an open house instead of scheduling a private showing. Learn how to easily identify serious buyers and create a system for identifying hot leads. This will save you time and energy and lead to fewer disappointments.

8. Have a Marketing Budget

A business requires investment. Having a clear budget for marketing – whether for social media ads, professional videos, or print materials – will make your path to success smoother. You can adjust the budget as needed, but creating one and sticking to it will guide you as you build your business.

9. First Impressions Matter

Your first impression is your last impression. You never get a second chance to make a good first impression, so when the opportunity arises, make sure to leave a great one.

By following these tips, you'll not only become a better agent but also a more successful one. Remember, it's about building trust, staying persistent, and never stopping your improvement.

"

YOU NEVER GET A SECOND CHANCE TO MAKE A GOOD FIRST IMPRESSION, SO WHEN THE OPPORTUNITY ARISES, MAKE SURE TO LEAVE A GREAT ONE.

"

PROSPECTING

Back to Basics: The Power of Door Knocking in Real Estate

Door knocking is just one of the strategies we use to meet people and get listings. Things don't always go as planned. A home isn't truly ZOLD unless it's unconditional and the deposit has been paid. If it's a conditional sale, it can sometimes fall out of contract. Clients can betray you, and we all have tough moments.

I've found that the best way for me to adjust my attitude is to go back to my roots. If I need a boost, I return to what brought me success in the early days of my career – knocking on doors and meeting people.

The Phone Approach

Cold Calls

A good agent is also a good prospector. The more comfortable you become with prospecting and cold calling, the better you get at handling objections, which leads to listing more properties and doubling your income. Keep in mind, practise makes perfect.

The purpose of the phone call is to secure the appointment, not to sell the product. Providing too much information upfront can cause your prospect to feel they can make a decision without hearing your full presentation. This is not what you want. Therefore, a well-planned approach will serve you better.

Cold Calling Script Example:

'Hi, this is Zed calling from Z. Real Estate. How are you today? The reason for my call is to inform you that I'll be in your area on Tuesday, offering homeowners a free, up-to-date market valuation. Would you like to take advantage of this service? I'd love to stop by and introduce myself. My company will contact you on Tuesday morning, say at 9 or 11 o'clock?'

There will be objections or negotiations over the phone, and you can check the list of answers in our Objection Handling section. However, it is important to remember that the goal is to get the appointment.

The Cold Approach in Person

In the real estate business, you will occasionally have the opportunity to stop by and see a prospect in person. This is called a cold call in person.

Here are some of my effective rules for you to follow:

- **Know the Name**: Always know the name of the person you're calling or want to meet. Don't walk in and ask for the store owner or manager – do your homework. If you must, stop outside the store's door and ask who owns the store.
- **Get to Know Your Local Businesses**: Your job is to get to know every shop owner and café owner in your area. Make sure your business cards are displayed in their retail shops.
- **Eliminate Objections**: This approach is used to set an appointment and eliminate the objections. It's much easier than cold calling on the phone because selling in person is more effective.

Make sure you've practised your scripts and dialogues first with colleagues and have done enough role-plays before approaching potential clients. You only get one chance to leave a good impression.

LISTING PRESENTATION

Refine Your Pitch

Start with a Brief Introduction of Yourself and the Company

Vendors want an agent who is confident in what they can do and can explain how they do it, giving specific examples.

Show them your video testimonials or your best property video at the start to build credibility. When giving a brief introduction of your skills, here are a few things that must be mentioned to capture their attention right from the start:

- How many homes you've ZOLD in their area in the past 12 months
- What types of homes you've ZOLD (if they were similar to theirs)
- How quickly you've ZOLD homes listed with you
- How much over reserve you have achieved

Remember, they focus on the end numbers. Be realistic and over-deliver, but never over-promise.

Get to Know Your Potential Vendor

After your brief introduction, take a few minutes to get to know your potential vendors better. Taking the time at this stage to get to know them encourages communication, helps you angle your pitch to their needs, and puts the homeowners at ease.

Practise your pitch perfectly before meeting your clients. They will judge you on everything – from your presentation, handshake, smile, and body language.

Questions to Ask Your Homeowners

Get to know your vendors as much as possible, ask as many questions as you can, and make it about them.

- Why are you moving?
- When do you need to move?
- Where are you moving to?
- Have you already found a home there?
- Is getting a good price or timing more important for you?
- What will you do if your home doesn't sell?

- What are you looking for in a listing agent?
- How much is left on your mortgage?
- Do you have a mortgage broker?
- Are you building a new home?
- Do you have a solicitor?
- Are there any easements, caveats, or covenants on the land?
- Are there any issues with the home that we need to be aware of?

Knowing this information will help you deliver a pitch that helps them move to their next phase of life. For example, if someone has already made an offer on a home at another location, they might need to sell their current home quickly.

You can use this information to explain how it will take much longer to sell their home if it is priced too high.

"

PRACTISE YOUR PITCH PERFECTLY
BEFORE MEETING YOUR CLIENTS.

"

Explain the Process (Auction or Private Sale)

The big question faced by all sellers:

Auction or Private Sale? You have to explain the process step by step:

- Appraisal process
- Open for inspection
- Your communication/feedback

- Negotiations and what to expect
- The closing process

Remember, either you close them or they close you.

Explain the method you will use to market their home. Explain the differences between auction and private sale. Spend time educating them on the entire process. Elaborate on how the sales process works.

There are pros and cons to both methods. The more your vendors know what happens behind the scenes, the better you can connect with them, and the higher your chances are of winning the listing.

Present Your CMA (Comparable Sales)

Include recent sales in the area or current homes on the market for sale that are similar to the home you're doing a presentation for. Show historic trends along with information on how quickly homes are selling in their area and the average days on market for a property.

Be sure to explain how and why you picked your comparisons as well as any other details of how you arrived at the price for their home. This helps the vendors understand the price range you'll set for their home.

Go Through Your Marketing Packages

Explain and educate them on the importance of marketing. The goal is to have enough buyers walk through the home to bring the best offer for a person's largest asset. This is where the money talks – you have to spend it to make it. A wise investment will take you far.

Staging and Declutter

If a seller's home is vacant, you can explain the benefits of staging and decluttering. Make sure you have experience or contacts in this area. Include photos of before and after staging in your listing presentation.

Contact the interior designer while you're doing your presentation and book a time right then and there to start the process.

AGENT'S PRICE OPINION: MASTERING REAL ESTATE PRICING AND NEGOTIATION

Many people want to complicate the process of selling a house, but successful real estate sales boil down to three factors:

1. ABP – Always Be Publicising.
2. Show a property to its full advantage.
3. Know how to close the deal.

You don't need to throw a fancy party or take a buyer on a helicopter ride to sell a property. The three main things to focus on are important for success. Remember, real estate is not complicated.

However, everything depends on pricing the home correctly. People often believe their home is worth more than it really is, no matter if it's a small apartment or a luxury home. It's natural for sellers to think their home is special and worth more than the market value.

It can be tough to tell sellers the reality – that their home may not be worth as much as they think. Sellers usually want to go with the real estate agent who gives them the highest price estimate because it validates their emotional connection to the home. But it's important to be honest and realistic.

When faced with this situation, I tell the homeowner that I can give them what they want to hear and take the listing, but my priority is building long-term relationships and making people happy.

A property is only worth whatever someone is willing to pay for it. It's true, the market dictates what a house is worth; today's buyers are more knowledgeable than ever as they have access to all the necessary information online. You don't need an agent to tell you what you want to hear, you need someone to tell you what you need to hear. You hire an agent on the basis of their negotiation and marketing skills or how much of a go-getter they are.

Any good agent can tell you what sold at what price, but a great agent will be educating the client as to why the properties sold at that price. The 'why' can be just as important as the 'how much?'.

The key to finding your seller's most accurate price is to know the stories of the outliers – those homes that sold above or below the norm.

For instance, the neighbours to the north might have sold their home cheaply to a friend who was bailing them out of financial trouble. The neighbours to the south might have got higher than what the market would bear because it was the buyer's childhood home and they wanted it at any price. Just like me, the house I'm living in now – I bought it for $170,000 more than the house I sold next door to mine because I wanted to be in that location. I believe when you're buying a place of principle, $100k to $250k in the long term doesn't really make a difference. You will make that money via capital improved value anyway, and you can always refinance if you have bought well. But if you're buying an investment property, every dollar and every cent counts.

An agent's credibility depends on understanding all aspects of what goes into pricing a home. That way, I'm able to answer a seller who doesn't understand why their home isn't worth as much as the house down the street was.

CLOSE MORE DEALS WITH A POSITIVE ATTITUDE

Focus on the Solution, Not the Problem

Mindset is everything in sales, especially in how you react to problems. You can solve anything you want in life as long as it has nothing to do with your health. I personally don't believe in stress, depression, anxiety, or bad energy. If you're stressed and under pressure, book a ticket and go away for a week – come back fresh. People can feel your energy and enthusiasm, so be so focused on your goals that there's no time to waste on anything but making sales and winning.

As a salesman, you must always focus on the solution. Start thinking about how you can clarify the situation, find out why things went wrong, give options to resolve the issue, and work towards an outcome. By having a solutions-focused mindset, you become proactive in your approach when things don't go according to plan.

Start Your Day with Positive Thoughts

Be grateful. When you wake up in the morning, take a few breaths and take time to find something you are grateful for. Give thanks to the people who love you for who you are. How you start the morning sets the tone for the rest of the day.

"

PEOPLE CAN FEEL YOUR ENERGY AND ENTHUSIASM,
SO BE SO FOCUSED ON YOUR GOALS.

"

THE PERFECT PITCH: HOW TO WIN PEOPLE IN THE FIRST 10 MINUTES

When it comes to Zelling your pitch isn't what you think it is. It's not just the presentation or the price – it's what happens in the first ten minutes of your meeting.

That's when people decide, deep down, whether they're in or out. After that, you're not really pitching anymore – you're negotiating. They've already made a decision. Now they're just working out the terms.

A pitch is simply you offering something – an idea, a service, a solution – in hopes that someone will give you their time, money, or trust in return. Whether you're selling a home, asking for a raise, or even asking someone out on a date... it's all a pitch.

And guess what? We pitch ourselves every day – to clients, to colleagues, to loved ones.

It's not always easy. Pitching takes confidence, clarity, and the ability to make someone feel something. The better you are at it, the more successful you'll be – not just in business, but in life.

Every pitch is a chance to leave someone better than you found them. That's the real win – not just closing the deal, but elevating the person in front of you.

If you can do that consistently, they'll say yes. Not because you pressured them – but because you made them believe in what's next.

The Bottom Line: Get clear on what they want. Help them visualise the better version of themselves. Make the experience unforgettable. And most importantly – make them feel something.

That's how you master the art of the pitch.

ZED'S PITCH PERFECT

Let's make it happen for you! Whether you're selling vacuums door-to-door, pitching for a bigger position in your company, or selling homes, let's make your pitch perfect.

Remember your first job interview? That's a pitch. I remember mine very well – my dream job. I was 19 years old, and I had never put on a proper suit before. I was so nervous walking in, stepping into that grand marble foyer which had once been a train station. I had been up half the night. I remember my heart beating so loudly I thought people could hear it. Looking back, I realised I made the mistake pretty much everyone makes before any big meeting or interview. I built it up the night before to be this huge, monumental thing. That's not the mistake. The mistake, I now realise, was that I was going it alone!

Here's what I've realised happens to most people before a big meeting: They isolate themselves. They close the world out and run things over and over through their heads.

I've now learnt to do something with someone before my shoots and pitches. It leaves me more relaxed and helps me make a seamless transition.

Have you ever been on a date, or pitched something, or tried to sell something, and it didn't go so well? You look back and wonder, *Why in the world was I so boring? I'm never boring when I am with my best friend; that's when I am fun, relaxed, and myself.*

Well, that's the point: You want to be exactly like you are with your best friend.

In any interview setting, it's an audition. You want that role! No one wants ordinary. Remember what sets you apart and play that up because anyone you're meeting with – interviewer, homebuyer, tax assessor, your boss – is hearing from people all day long. So what sets you apart? I'll walk in the room backward and wear flashy socks if it makes them laugh. My theory is that if you entertain yourself, your charisma will be so appealing that you'll get the part. If you don't get the part, it wasn't the right thing for you anyway, and you had fun losing it to someone boring.

THE SECRETS OF PERSUASIVE SELLING

Here's how I use a simple technique to sell someone on a great house and investment. A buyer emails me to see one of my listings. I immediately respond, 'Calling you shortly'. Just like that. I don't say yes or no. I leave the buyer waiting for my call.

Establish Credibility.

The pitch has already begun. I leave a few minutes, just enough for the buyer to be drawn into my little world. My email signature provides a link to look at my profile, social media pages, and my latest press mentions, as seen on Channels 9, 7, and 10. Before I call, the buyer hopefully picks up from my email signature that I am 'The number one agent in Victoria in 2021 by *Herald Sun*'. The future ZOLD has already started – before we have spoken and before the buyer has seen the property.

Create Urgency While Saying Positive Things.

I then call the buyer and open up with great energy. We talk about when to see the home, and I mention I have three private showings there the day after tomorrow for other buyers who have been waiting for a home in this neighbourhood. They will definitely want to get in before them.

Boost Confidence In a Conversation.

Meet outside the home, and in the driveway to the home, I speak about the market in general. This is my opportunity to say that the market is on fire (if true) and how I ZOLD $40 million in deals in less than 6 weeks, my best month ever! I might add there are a lot of Chinese, all-cash buyers lately, and I ask the buyer why he thinks that is.

Establish a Friendly Dream While Creating a Little More Urgency.

I open the door to the home and start showing him around, talking about the seller's attention to detail. I make the seller seem personal and relatable. I explain how much love has gone into the home and how difficult it is for the seller to now part with it and this amazing area. I have one goal: to get the buyer not only comfortable but also obsessed with the neighbourhood, the home, and me. We are friends now. We like each other. You must do this with whatever you're selling. So, the pitch doesn't start and end where it is obvious: it starts with you at the very first point of contact, whatever that is.

From the first seconds of our contact (via email), he was able to see he's in the hands of someone at the top of his game. In our two-minute phone call, I let him know I'm impressed that he's on his game and he's going to get to see the home before anyone else. In the thirty-second drive to the home, I talked about how hot the market is and fired him up. As we walked in the door, I began immediately pointing out details and the seller's amazing taste. I asked questions, made him feel at home, and at the same time collected information, and told him we have multiple people interested in it; people always want things they can't have so you take it away from them and it makes them want it even more.

Everybody wants what everybody wants. He started talking numbers. And we never discussed a single other house.

THE ZED WAY: WIN MORE LISTINGS, UNDERSTAND YOUR CLIENTS' NEEDS, AND BUILD STRONG RELATIONSHIPS

At every listing appraisal, I talk with the seller about coming together to agree on a price for listing their property. But before starting that conversation, I ask the seller many questions to learn more about them. What things matter to them? How do they live? What's important in their life? Knowing these things helps me serve them better. Instead of talking about myself, I focus on gathering information during our first chat.

Once I have all the answers, we move on to deciding the price.

While I have an idea about the prices of similar homes in the area, I don't share my thoughts right away. Pricing a home is like a strategic game, so I prefer to understand what other agents have suggested before giving my opinion. This way, I can propose a fair price without risking the listing.

I always make sure to know what other agents have said before deciding on a price. When talking with the seller, I ask about the properties they are comparing with their home. While some sellers may have an idea, they often just say, 'That's why you're here'. While they're not wrong, it can be difficult when they're not ready to share information.

Sellers often tend to favour the agent who suggests the highest price, but that can be a quick decision without proof that the home can actually sell for that amount. Starting with a price that's too high can harm the home's chances of selling quickly. It's important to generate interest in the first few weeks on the market, which won't happen if the price is too high.

While some overpriced properties can sell, it's not the usual outcome. Starting with a slightly lower price can often lead to competing offers from buyers. The key is to find the right balance to attract offers at or near the asking price. For instance, if a seller believes her home is worth $8 million, and other agents agree, I might feel that price is too high. In such cases, I remember a strategy called 'Expressions of interest' or 'sale by set date'.

After discussing the potential price with the seller, I then highlight my sales history and accomplishments to build trust. I explain how hands-on and available I am, assuring the seller they can reach me directly when necessary.

By anticipating and addressing potential concerns before they come up, I show sellers that I understand their needs and am prepared to offer solutions. Taking a proactive approach to answering questions can make my responses more dependable and beneficial to the seller.

In wrapping up, no salesperson is perfect, but we can set ourselves apart from the competition by acknowledging our mistakes first. Salespeople may feel hesitant to point out their weaknesses, hoping clients won't notice them. However, being upfront about our flaws shows confidence and honesty.

THE BLUEPRINT FOR ZELLING SUCCESS: PASSION, PREPARATION, AND PEOPLE

1. Love what you do, be passionate about what you do.
2. Know your product. Understanding population, demographics, fixtures, and fittings builds your credibility.
3. People say we get lucky, but I believe there's no such thing as luck. Luck is when preparation meets opportunity.
4. Create urgency on deals, pre-qualify, and work smart, not just hard. If you work both hard and smart, it's a bonus. You have to be available 24/7, regardless of the time or where you are.
5. Master your craft. Don't just stand at the door – sell every aspect of the house. Feel the floors,

touch the curtains, and perfect your pitch. Practice makes perfect. Plan, prepare, practise, perform, produce, party.

6. Surround yourself with the right people and the right culture. I hated the environment during the first three years of my career. I felt lost being surrounded by lost people. Remember, the speed of the boss or company is the speed of the employee.
7. Get a mentor. Surround yourself with a senior who can give you the right advice. I wouldn't have failed in the first three years of my career if I had a mentor.
8. Respect your clients and help everyone equally. As salespeople, we often dislike dealing with rental issues or leasing enquiries. But today's renter turns into tomorrow's buyer or seller. If you give the right advice, you'll always be remembered. For example, I recently helped a young kid by giving advice on how to flip properties, without expecting anything in return. Suddenly, I got a call from his dad, who turned out to be a developer and offered me projects to sell. Helping and giving starts the process of receiving.

PEOPLE DON'T LIKE BEING ZOLD, BECOME A FRIEND OR AN ADVISER.

Sales is about finding a sincere way to connect with people. If you want your clients to do continuous business with you and invest their money, you must make them feel comfortable with your ability to get them what they want. People don't like being ZOLD, but they love hearing success stories. You should always do more than what you've been paid for – it's not always about making money right away. It doesn't work like that. People can smell a salesman from a mile away.

No matter what you sell, spouting facts and pointing out components of a product isn't what inspires someone to open their wallet.

Steve Jobs said it best: 'People don't know what they want until you show it to them'.

Closing a deal is about tapping into emotions. The sooner you can take off the 'salesman's hat' and get in tune with your client's emotions and desires, the better you'll become at working the deal. If you're not sure how to do that, remember this: what makes an exceptional salesperson is someone who works for the deal.

“

YOU MUST USE YOUR KNOWLEDGE, ADVICE, AND EXPERTISE TO CONNECT A CUSTOMER WITH THE PRODUCT THAT BEST FITS THEIR NEEDS.

”

Never start off by talking about the product. Always make a connection first. Give them a genuine compliment or ask a question to start the conversation. Get a 'yes' and a smile. Once that connection is made, you can ease into talking about your product. If you're shy, think of approaching new customers as you would a potential new friend. At one time, your best friend was a total stranger. At some point, you met, made a connection, and now you know their deep, dark secrets.

The point is, with anything I do, I always focus on building rapport and relationships first – and then I Zell my pitch.

If you want to be truly productive, give yourself a target. Meet at least ten new people every day and get their contact info. Start with just one if you need to, but get in the habit of making friends everywhere you go.

A salesperson's network of contacts is their currency. Think of meeting people as money. Meeting ten people a day for a year is like depositing 3,650 'people dollars' into your bank that you wouldn't otherwise have. The more connections you make, the more business you'll do.

OVERCOMING EMOTIONS, NOT WALLETS: THE KEY TO ZELLING SUCCESS

I ZOLD a place to a couple in an area they never imagined themselves living in, and it was way over their budget. How did I do it? I ZOLD them the lifestyle. I asked, 'Can you imagine how good it would feel to live just ten doors down from the bay?'

Sales isn't just about numbers or features; it's about tapping into emotions and painting a picture that resonates with your clients' desires and dreams.

Salespeople who consistently close deals:

- Are relentless in their pursuit of opportunities.
- Show empathy by understanding their clients' needs and aspirations.
- Demonstrate patience because building trust takes time.
- Actively listen to uncover what truly matters to their clients.
- Consistently bring value through insights, expertise, and solutions.
- Treat clients with respect, regardless of their circumstances.

In sales, you can't always negotiate with someone's wallet, but you can negotiate with their feelings. Tap into their emotions, show them the possibilities, and you'll find a way to make the deal happen.

CONFIDENCE CLOSES: WHY PEOPLE BUY YOU BEFORE THE PROPERTY

People don't just buy the property. They buy into you.

If you want someone to buy what you're Zelling, your confidence needs to ooze out of your pores.

Deliver your pitch with energy, passion, and belief because real estate isn't just about properties. It's about people.

Your vibe is your advantage. And confidence is what sets the tone.

You have to decide that there's no option but to be the BEST salesperson the world has ever seen.

Confidence isn't about being arrogant. It's about being committed. When you're next pitching a home, negotiating a deal, or trying to win a listing – don't just show up. Show up like you're the best in the game.

Speak like you believe it. Sell like it's already ZOLD.

"

DELIVER YOUR PITCH WITH ENERGY, PASSION, AND BELIEF.

"

MASTER THE ART OF LISTENING: THE KEY TO TRANSFORMATIONAL ZELLING

Listen to your clients before you talk. Take a few seconds to digest what they are saying before you respond. Think about their words, and be sincere when you speak. There is nothing worse than spouting a line just to fill the silence.

I've been to many listing presentations with agents over the years, and one of the biggest problems I've observed is that they don't truly listen to what the client wants. Instead, they push the client to go on the market and sell a marketing package that benefits the agent rather than addressing the client's actual needs. When a client isn't motivated or is saying one thing while the agent is focused solely on closing the deal for their own benefit, it's a recipe for failure.

Use this Formula: **Ask = Acknowledge = Ask**

I use this formula to build rapport and relationships. Be transformational, not transactional. Storytelling is what sells, and mastering it is essential.

Model yourself after an Academy Award winner! Great actors deliver scripted lines in a way that feels fresh and genuine. They take the audience on an emotional journey – whether it's tears, fear, or laughter.

I'm not telling you to put on a character – you must be genuine. But don't be afraid to dig deep and show sympathy. That's how a good salesperson ensures they are giving the client what they need to end the story with a big sale.

Nine Reasons Why This Formula Works:

1. Acknowledging opens the door to genuine connections. It helps you feel more comfortable and secure when talking to new people.
2. Acknowledging helps you think quickly on your feet. You'll be able to come up with solutions to problems or objections almost instantly.
3. It trains your brain to focus on YES. Not making a deal or not reaching a positive outcome is no longer an option.
4. It helps you identify your strengths and weaknesses. Practising this formula sharpens your skills and reveals areas for improvement.
5. You learn to relate to your 'scene partner'. Ultimately, every deal is just another scene, and your client is your partner.

6. Acknowledging forces you to listen before you react. Truly hearing what your clients want is key to closing sales.
7. It allows you to control the narrative. When you master this skill, you can guide the direction of your deals.
8. Acknowledging helps conquer shyness. It builds confidence and makes you more effective at engaging with clients.
9. ZOLD. Because when you connect, listen, and acknowledge, closing the deal becomes inevitable.

By using Ask = Acknowledge = Ask, you're not just selling – you're building trust, relationships, and ultimately, success. Listen first, respond with authenticity, and watch how your Zelling transforms.

ZELLING WITH ENTHUSIASM AND EXPERTISE: THE KEY TO WINNING CLIENTS

When it comes to showing homes to buyers in real estate, your enthusiasm and expertise can make all the difference.

As you walk through each property, let your passion for real estate shine through. Share your in-depth knowledge of the market trends, neighbourhood perks, and property features with your clients. By combining your excitement for the homes you show with your expert guidance, you create a memorable and impactful experience for potential buyers. Your enthusiasm will naturally captivate them, while your expertise reassures them that they are in capable hands. This winning combination not only helps you stand out as a real estate professional but also builds trust and rapport with your clients.

So, keep that enthusiasm high, leverage your expertise, and watch as your clients are not just impressed but inspired to find their dream home with you by their side.

Always be Zelling, even when you don't have a deal to close. Remember, you are your product, and you must present yourself accordingly. You don't have to be rich to be polished, professional, and proactive, but embodying these qualities will propel you towards success.

ZELLING WITH HEART

A strong and motivated salesperson can sell anything, as selling is not just about the product itself.

It's easy to learn about the product you're selling, but to really succeed in sales, you need to understand the people you're selling to. What do they want? What are their goals and needs? What kind of vibe are they giving off? Don't stop providing great service once the sale is made. You need to maintain the relationship because in real estate, it's all about the connection with your clients. Your success depends on keeping up that good relationship. Once the deal is done, clients can choose to work with another agent, so it's important to show them you care by staying in touch. This helps you earn their business again when they're ready to buy or sell a home, and also leads to referrals from them in the future.

You also have to adapt to different situations. It's vital for the buyer to trust you and believe in your knowledge about the product you're selling. For instance, if you're selling fabric, you need to know if it will shrink or stretch and if the colour will fade. Be ready to answer any questions they might have.

Listening is imperative. And this means that sometimes, you need to stop talking and simply listen. Clients want to feel like their opinions matter. Understanding their needs is essential to moving forward. Many salespeople miss this, and as a result, they struggle to understand their customers, which can lead to problems.

Be passionate about what you're selling. If you don't naturally love what you're selling, find something about it that drives you beyond just making money. And always, always, stay calm under pressure. When faced with difficult situations or criticism, like being yelled at by older clients, remain composed and address their concerns. It's important not to let negative feedback affect you and to handle it professionally. This experience taught me a lot about sales, and dealing with challenges became easier over time.

ZED'S SALES TIPS: ELEVATING YOUR APPROACH

The way you approach sales and your potential customers will form a lot of your success, or otherwise. I've included these tips so that you can elevate your approach to selling and building a customer base:

- When you pay attention to your appearance and incorporate the environment and community into the way you dress, clients will be able to envision themselves in that atmosphere.

- The bigger your digital network and social media following are, the greater outreach you'll have, especially with younger generations.
- Building a brand and a trusted name takes a long time, and it only takes one mistake to destroy it. That's why you have to treat your reputation like gold.
- By creating extraordinary experiences for your clients, you're not only promoting the properties you're selling but also effectively exposing your clients to the lifestyle they're seeking.
- Sometimes, you have to give people the opportunity to do things that may seem foreign to you, as there are exceptions to almost every rule.
- Keep an open mind. By considering different situations, you can handle any outcome.
- To attract high-end clients, you need to be active in the market. Know who's looking to buy, who's selling, and where the influential people live.
- Experts can be wrong. The more you learn about your industry, the better you can challenge ideas that don't seem right.
- Being knowledgeable is important, but don't act like you know everything. Just like honesty, it's good to admit when you don't know something.
- Getting to know people – regardless of who they are – is the best way to grow your personal and

professional networks. Always be open to meeting new people.

- Staying calm is a valuable skill, especially in sales and service.
- Don't just stay busy for the sake of it. Make sure everything you do is efficient and achieves results.
- Think quickly during stressful times, or else things can go wrong.

MASTERING PRODUCT KNOWLEDGE FOR SUCCESS IN SALES

A sales representative who doesn't fully understand the product they are selling is not effective. Learning about the product should be one of the first things you focus on before going to any appointments. You should be able to explain clearly how each product works, the value it brings to businesses, and why it appeals to your company's ideal customers.

You can't walk into a home without knowing the comparable sales in the area. The first step is to educate yourself before visiting a property in Brighton. Look online to find out who named the suburb, what the average house price and unit price is, the demographics of the area, land value, and building costs (like standard, mid-range, and high-end luxury). If you're not sure about any of this, sit down with your director and ask questions. You also need to learn how to do feasibility reports on development sites.

CLOSE FASTER

1. **Identify the Decision-maker.** In any industry, knowing the decision-maker is key to closing quickly. In my experience, it's often the wife, but always make sure you're addressing the right person who holds the final say.
2. **Be Real.** Always be the best, authentic version of yourself. Share your true self with the world in an honest way. People appreciate sincerity and will connect with you more when you're real with them.
3. **Create a Sense of Urgency.** Give your prospects a time frame to make a decision – whether it's two hours or 24 hours if it's a big deal. This urgency will encourage them to take action rather than delay.
4. **Overcome Objections.** When you hear an objection, your first instinct might be to jump in and respond immediately. However, stay calm, take a deep breath, and respond thoughtfully. Always do your homework so you can address their concerns effectively.
5. **Know Your Competition.** A comparative market analysis (CMA) is crucial. Know what your competitors are offering and make sure you're one step ahead. Personally, I often compete with myself and focus on being better than I was yesterday. Also, be mindful of what you say – knowledge is power.

By applying these strategies, you'll close deals faster and build stronger client relationships. Always be prepared, stay confident, and keep learning.

A CAREER IN REAL ESTATE

BEFORE STARTING A REAL ESTATE CAREER

Before you begin a career in real estate where you only earn based on sales, remember it will be a minimum of 90 days before settlement. Ask yourself these important questions:

- Are you outgoing?
- Are you passionate about properties?
- Are you willing to be a student or a follower? Big difference which I will explain a bit later in the coming chapters.
- Are you interested?
- Are you friendly and like to be around people?
- Do you have enough money to support yourself before you start making sales? And if not, are you ready to give up some things while you're learning?

If you answered no to any of these questions, this might not be the right job for you.

FIFTY PERCENT OF WINNING HAPPENS BEFORE YOU EVEN START

Simply put, you become what you think about.

Why do real estate agents fail? Because they think they will.

Do you have a positive attitude? Everyone will say yes, but fewer than one in 1,000 actually do. That's one-tenth of one percent. Are you really in that small percentile?

To find out, all you have to do is pass this simple test.

	Yes	No
I watch the news for at least one hour per day.		
I read the paper every day.		
I read a news magazine every week.		
I sometimes have a bad day that lasts all day.		
My job feels like a drag.		
I get angry for an hour or more.		
I talk to and commiserate with negative people.		
I look to blame others when something goes wrong.		
When something goes wrong, I tell others about it.		
I get angry at my spouse and don't speak for more than four hours.		
I bring personal problems to work and discuss them.		
I expect and plan for the worst.		
Bad weather affects my mood enough that I feel the need to comment on it.		

How did you score?

- 0–2 Yes answers: You have a positive attitude.
- 3–6 Yes answers: You have a negative attitude.
- 7 or more Yes answers: You may like to seek professional advice from a counsellor.

If you received more than four Yes responses, I suggest you invest in the books, recordings, and teachings of Jim Rohn, Dale Carnegie,

Napoleon Hill, and Earl Nightingale. These are the people who will show you how you can, and why you must stop telling yourself you can't.

Here's Where It Gets Real

Several national studies have revealed the following startling statistics about why salespeople fail:

- 15% – Inadequate training in both product knowledge and sales skills.
- 20% – Poor verbal and written communication skills.
- 15% – A difficult or unsupportive manager.
- 50% – Attitude.

Sounds almost impossible, doesn't it? Agents could succeed 50 percent more simply by changing the way they think. Earl Nightingale, in his legendary recording The Strangest Secret, reveals the key: 'We become what we think about'. But it is a dedicated discipline that must be practised every single day.

Want to Start Changing Your Attitude?

A change in your attitude will have a miraculous effect on your success and your income. Live these thoughts and exercises daily:

- When something goes wrong, recognise that the responsibility starts with you.
- You always have – and have always had – a choice.
- If you believe it's okay, it is. If you believe it's not, it isn't.
- Ignore the noise. Work on a worthwhile project, make a plan, or do something that moves your real estate business forward.

- For one year, read only positive books and material.
- When you face an obstacle, look for the opportunity inside it.
- Listen to motivational recordings, attend seminars, and invest in continuing education.
- Ignore anyone who tells you that you can't or tries to discourage you.
- Check your language. Is your glass half full or half empty? Partly cloudy or partly sunny? Eliminate the words can't and won't from your vocabulary.
- Talk about what you like – your clients, your work, your family. Not what you don't.
- Help others without keeping score. If you say 'I won't because they won't' – who loses? You do.
- How long do you stay in a bad mood? If it's more than five minutes, something needs to change.
- Count your blessings every single day.

If you took the hour a day you currently spend watching the news and converted it into positive action – learning, prospecting, or building your real estate business – at the end of one year you would have gained more than 15 full 24-hour days.

Which will help your career more: 15 days a year watching the news, or 15 days a year building your future?

The choice is yours.

Are You Born to Sell Real Estate? No – You Learn to Earn!

You've heard it, and you've probably said it: 'That agent is a natural'. Wrong. That is one of the biggest myths in real estate sales. Selling is a science – an acquired skill. The agent you thought was a natural painstakingly developed the traits and characteristics to succeed, then went about learning and applying the science of selling.

Take this personal inventory test. These are 21 traits and characteristics of great real estate agents. How many do you have?

Important note: There is a middle ground between yes and no. It's called 'working on it'. You're better off marking no until you've truly achieved that characteristic.

CHARACTERISTICS	YES	NO
I have set my goals in writing.		
I have good self-discipline.		
I am self-motivated.		
I want to be more knowledgeable.		
I want to build lasting client relationships.		
I am self-confident.		
I like myself.		
I love people.		
I love a challenge.		
I love to win.		
I can accept rejection with a positive attitude.		

CHARACTERISTICS	YES	NO
I can handle the details of a complex transaction.		
I am loyal to my clients and my word.		
I am enthusiastic.		
I am observant.		
I am a good listener.		
I am perceptive.		
I am a skilful communicator.		
I am a hard worker.		
I want to be financially secure.		
I am persistent.		

How did you score?

- 15 or more *honest* Yes answers: You have what it takes to build a thriving real estate career.
- 10 to 14: It could go either way. Your odds improve significantly if you answered yes to knowledge, enthusiasm, self-confidence, perception, self-motivation, and persistence.
- Under 10: Real estate sales may not be the right fit, regardless of the market opportunity in front of you.

Z.Talk: Not one of the traits above mentions closing deals or overcoming objections. The science of selling real estate can be learned and applied by anyone who embodies these characteristics. All you have to do is believe you can do it, commit yourself fully, and hold yourself to the standard you set.

What's Wrong With This Sale? It's You!

In 15 years of being in the real estate industry, I've never had an agent come up to me and say, 'I didn't close the deal and it was entirely my fault'.

Agents make the fatal mistake of blaming market conditions, interest rates, or unqualified buyers for their own inability to create a buying atmosphere. That mistake carries double jeopardy: you're blaming the wrong party, and you issue blame instead of taking responsibility – failing to see the urgent need for self-improvement.

I've identified 12.5 fatal flaws of real estate sales. Rate yourself honestly. Grab a red pen and mark an 'F' next to every flaw you need to work on.

1. You're Too Eager to Please.

Agents are too eager to please without securing a commitment or adding value.

The Move: When you send a listing presentation, book the follow-up appointment at the same time. When a buyer requests a showing, ask where they are in the decision-making process.

2. You're Talking When You Should Be Listening.

Does a doctor tell you where he went to medical school before examining you? No. He asks, 'Where does it hurt?'

The Move: Ask compelling questions – ones that uncover pain, emotion, and motivation. Ask questions your competing agents never think to ask.

3. You're Closing on a Handshake.

Nothing is more fatal than a client believing more was promised than you intended. When a seller says, 'I thought you said you'd cover the staging costs…' Whatever follows is a problem.

The Move: Write down and repeat back every promise, term, and expectation – every single time.

4. You're Trash-Talking the Competition.

Sure, the other broker may be terrible. What's your point? When you put them down, you only degrade yourself.

The Move: Always refer to competing agents as 'my worthy competition' or simply 'the industry standard'.

5. You're Checking in Instead of Adding Value.

Calling to ask, 'Did you get the comparable market analysis I sent?' or 'Do you have any questions?' makes you look like a pest, not a professional.

The Move: Call with value – a new listing that just hit the market, a neighbourhood insight, or a smart question.

6. You're Negotiating Against Yourself.

Asking, 'What will it take to earn your business?' is the single worst question in real estate sales. It will always lead to reduced commissions, unrealistic demands, and a loss of respect.

The Move: Instead, say, 'I'd love a brief opportunity to share why some of my clients chose me – even though I wasn't the agent offering the lowest commission.'

7. You're Walking in Blind.

Your prospect has likely already heard something about you, your brokerage, or your market approach – and it may not be accurate.

The Move: Ask first, 'What has your experience been with agents so far?' or 'How would you describe what you're looking for in representation?'

8. You're Pitching to Someone Who's Already Decided.

Your reputation may have preceded you. A buyer may have already chosen another agent, or may already want to work with you and is simply using your presentation to confirm – not decide.

The Move: Build rapport quickly before diving into your pitch. Ask directly where they are on the decision-making scale.

9. You're Calling to Check on Your Commission.

Follow-up calls are often just thinly veiled attempts to check on your commission. 'Have you made a decision yet?' is not a strategy.

The Move: After a listing presentation or buyer consultation, that follow-up window is your best opportunity to shine. Share a relevant market update, a helpful article, or a creative solution to their specific situation.

10. You're Arguing Instead of Proving.

An objection simply means: 'You haven't fully sold me yet, but I'm still interested'.

The Move: Use client testimonials to overcome objections – past sellers who got above asking, buyers who found their home in a tough market. If you must respond directly, ask thoughtful questions rather than making defensive statements.

11. You're Letting Price Do All the Talking.

If your entire value proposition comes down to commission rate or list price, you've already lost. Clients don't just hire an agent – they hire a strategy.

The Move: Be prepared to clearly articulate what you do differently at every stage of the transaction, from marketing to negotiation to closing.

12. You're Selling Features Instead of Outcomes.

Telling a seller their home will be on realestate.com and domain.com is not a marketing plan – every agent does that. Clients want to know what result they're going to get, not what tools you use.

The Move: Shift every conversation from 'here's what I do' to 'here's what you'll experience and walk away with'.

12.5. You Think the Deal Is Done When the Contract is Signed. The transaction doesn't end at the offer – it ends at the closing table. Agents who disappear after the contract is executed lose referrals, reviews, and repeat business.

The Move: Stay visible, communicative, and proactive from contract to close. That last half mile is where your reputation is made.

The agents who close the most deals aren't the ones with the best listings – they're the ones who take an honest look in the mirror.

THE BRIDGE BETWEEN POSITIVE AND NEGATIVE

In real estate, most agents focus on what can't get done rather than what can. They handicap themselves mentally by saying, 'I can't get the seller on the phone. Nobody returns my calls. I can't find qualified buyers. I overslept. I forgot. I didn't write it down. Nobody told me'. And then they slide into full excuse mode: 'I didn't have enough time'. Or worse – 'I'm doing the best I can'.

Think about how you'd feel if a colleague walked into your office and laid all of that on you. Would you want to listen, or would you want to avoid that person at all costs? The answer is obvious.

But there is a better answer, and it lives in your ability to choose your perspective. If you focus on the negative, the results will almost certainly be negative. If you focus on positive anticipation and positive outcomes, positive results will follow. It really is that simple – and that difficult.

Here are eight things you can do every day to maintain the focus, intensity, drive, and commitment needed to shift your direction from 'Woe is me' to 'Whoa, what a life!'

1. Stop Blaming Circumstances for Your Results.

It's not the market, the interest rates, the inventory, or the economy – it's you. You have a choice in everything you do. Choose a better way. Don't blame the path; change the path. Don't blame the market; change your approach to it. Top producers close deals in every market condition. The circumstances are the same for everyone. The difference is the agent.

2. Stop Blaming Other People for Your Situation.

Take full responsibility for yourself and your results. If you consistently find yourself pointing fingers at your broker, your leads, your clients, or your competitors, here's the hard truth: it isn't them. Get over it and get to work.

3. Know Your Clients and Prospects Better.

In real estate, knowledge is power – and knowing your prospect is just as valuable for preventing problems as it is for solving them. If you can't get a seller to return your call, that's on you for not establishing the right communication rhythm from the start. Know the best time to reach each person. Know when they're making their decision. Know their timeline, their motivation, and their concerns. Double-confirm every commitment and every appointment.

4. Persist Until You Get an Answer.

A serious buyer or seller will respect a tenacious agent. Research consistently shows it takes multiple touchpoints to earn a client's trust and business. Do you have what it takes to follow up five, seven, or ten times without giving up? Even a firm 'no' is valuable – at least you know where you stand and can redirect your energy accordingly.

5. Know Where You Are and Where You Need to Be.

Manage your time like a professional. Have lunch with a client, not just a friend. Keep detailed, accurate records of every prospect and every conversation. Know your pipeline well enough that follow-up becomes second nature rather than a scramble. Are you organised enough to reach the tenth touchpoint and still have the situation under enough control to close the deal?

6. Work on Your Skills Every Single Day.

Books, podcasts, seminars, market reports, negotiation training. You can never learn too much. I challenge you to invest one hour a day in your professional development. One hour a day, seven days a week, for one year equals more than nine full weeks of focused education. The next time you reach for the remote, ask yourself what you could be doing instead to sharpen your skills and strengthen your mindset.

7. Become Solution-Oriented.

Instead of dwelling on problems, spend that same energy finding solutions. This single shift in thinking has done more for successful careers in real estate than almost any other strategy. Every obstacle in this business – a deal falling through, a low appraisal, a difficult negotiation – contains an opportunity if you're looking for it. If you're too focused on the problem, the opportunity will pass you right by.

8. Think Before You Speak.

Agents often say things without thinking, only to regret them moments later – to a client, a cooperating agent, or a prospect. Before you engage anyone, pause for just a moment. How will your words land? What could you say instead that would create a more positive, productive response? The goal is always a positive outcome. This step requires the most self-discipline of all, but try it consistently and you will be amazed at the results.

ATTITUDE OPPORTUNITY

You've been handed a bag of cement and a bucket of water. You can use them to build a stumbling block – a wall that stops you cold – or you can use them to build a stepping stone: a bridge to wherever you want to go in this business and in your life.

The choice is yours. It has always been yours.

Are you missing opportunities in your real estate career because you are too busy staring at the obstacles?

YOUR BEST NEW PROSPECTS ARE YOUR PRESENT CLIENTS

Looking for new prospects? Who isn't! It may interest you to know that you already have hundreds of hot prospects you're not paying attention to.

They're your past and present clients.

Consider these 11 assets already working in your favour:

1. They know you.
2. They like you.
3. You have established rapport.
4. Confidence and trust have already been built.
5. You have a track record of delivering results.
6. They respect you.
7. They have experienced your service firsthand – and they liked it.
8. They will return your call.
9. They will be far more receptive to what you have to offer.
10. They have financial capacity and have done business with you before.
11. They don't need to be sold – they will buy.

Here are some ideas to get your present clients to do business with you again – now:

- **Introduce them to something new.** The market is always shifting, and new opportunities arise constantly. Share a new listing, a new neighbourhood gaining traction, or a new investment strategy with genuine enthusiasm. People love to be in the know. Create excitement about how the current market conditions present a unique opportunity specifically for them. Sell the vision. Then let them buy.
- **Sell them an upgrade or an enhancement.** Bigger, better, more space, better location, stronger return on investment.

Upgrading from a starter home to a forever home, or from a single-family investment property to a multi-unit building, has built tremendous wealth for real estate clients who had an agent proactive enough to bring them the opportunity. Upselling builds fortunes – just ask any top-producing agent who stays in touch with their database.

- **Sell them more of the same in a different place.** Look for other opportunities – a vacation property, an investment rental, a commercial space for their growing business, or a replacement property due to changing life circumstances. You may have to dig a little, but the soil is far softer with a past client than with the pile of rocks you typically face when cold-prospecting a stranger.
- **Introduce them to services they didn't know you offered.** You may have access to property management referrals, 1031 exchange resources, commercial real estate connections, or relocation services – and very few of your clients know about all of it. When a client says, 'Oh, I didn't know you could help with that', don't blame the client. Blame the agent for not communicating their full value.
- **Take them to lunch.** Getting a client out of their home or office often opens the door to conversations that never happen over the phone. You'll uncover life changes – a growing family, a job transition, a desire to invest – that signal a real estate need on the horizon. Ask them to bring someone who might be thinking about buying or selling. Bring a connection that could benefit them in return. Build the relationship and you'll build more sales.

- **Ask for one referral a month.** This is the true report card on the job you've done for your clients. If they trust you enough to refer you to a friend, family member, or colleague, you've done your job well. If they won't, that tells you something too.
- **Give them one referral a month.** Sending business to your clients – whether it's recommending their restaurant, their law firm, or their contracting company – creates a new dynamic in how they see you. You become more than their real estate agent. You become a valued connector. And people find ways to return that favour.

Z.Talk: Whether or not a conversation leads to an immediate transaction, staying consistently in front of your clients builds relationship equity and goodwill that pays dividends for years.

If you find yourself unable to call on your past clients, or if you come up with a convenient excuse like, 'I've already sold them a home – there's nothing left to offer', what that really means is one of the following:

1. You failed to establish deep enough rapport during the transaction.
2. You did not follow up well – or at all – after closing.

3. There may be an unresolved issue and you're avoiding the conversation.
4. You are in need of more sales training and creative thinking.
5. You never built a genuine relationship – you simply made a transaction.

Most agents believe that unless they're calling a client with an active listing or a live buyer, it's a wasted call. Nothing could be further from the truth.

I am consistently amazed by agents who close a deal and immediately move on to chase the next stranger – completely abandoning a client who, with just a little continued attention, would buy again, sell again, and refer everyone they know.

Take an honest look at your client list. I'll bet there are dozens – if not hundreds – of opportunities sitting right there, waiting for you to reach out.

I would rather have 100 loyal real estate clients than 1,000 cold leads any day of the week.

THE SECRET TO A WINNING WEEK

The secret to a great week is to use Monday as a springboard. Schedule your hottest prospect for Monday morning.

Make a sale on Monday. It does wonders for your week.

I'm often asked if there is some secret to consistent sales performance in real estate. The answer is simple: Have a great Monday and have a great Friday. How you perform on the first day of the week sets the tone for the rest of it. And how you do on Monday is based entirely on how smart you worked the week before. If you're disciplined enough to follow these methods, you won't believe the difference it will make in your productivity – and your commission checks.

If you're looking for consistency in your real estate sales performance, try these nine steps:

1. **Make a sale first thing Monday morning.** Set a listing appointment or buyer consultation for early Monday morning with a prospect you're confident is ready to move. Locking in a signed contract or agreement to start your week will give you an incredible mental boost and put you in motion to make another one.
2. **Talk to people.** Many clients and decision-makers hold internal meetings on Monday mornings, so make your time count with scheduled appointments. This is why many top-producing agents hold their team meetings on Tuesdays – to follow up on weekend open house leads and showing activity. Start making calls immediately after your meeting, and if time permits, call early. Serious buyers and sellers are often early risers.
3. **Learn something new.** Play a real estate training or motivational podcast in your car on the way to your first showing or listing appointment. Instead of listening to the same news or music, feed your mind with knowledge you can put to use within the hour. A new objection-handling technique learned at 8:00 am can be tested by 9:00 am.
4. **Set at least five appointments for the rest of the week.**

Why not have a Monday full of success and positive anticipation? It's entirely up to you. Pick up the phone and make it happen – buyer consultations, listing presentations, follow-up calls with fence-sitters.

5. **Work hard all week – especially on Friday.** How you finish the last day of the week sets the tone for the next one. Most agents slack off on Friday afternoon. If you work intensely instead, you'll ensure success next week and give yourself a real reason to enjoy the weekend.
6. **Continue your education throughout the week.** Consistently sharpening your real estate knowledge – market trends, negotiation strategies, contract details – is just as important as prospecting. Make sure you carve out learning time on Friday morning in particular.
7. **Make a sale on Friday afternoon.** Schedule a contract signing or closing call for Friday afternoon. There is nothing quite like ending the week on a positive note with a deal locked in.
8. **Confirm your Monday appointment on Friday.** If you worked hard the previous four days, you've already set your Monday morning make-a-sale appointment. Call that prospect on Friday to confirm and keep the momentum alive going into the weekend.
9. **Set at least five appointments for next week before you leave Friday.** Guarantee yourself a full schedule so you can spend your weekend recharging instead of worrying about an empty calendar. Make this commitment to yourself: 'I will not leave the office on Friday until I have

five appointments set and my Monday sale appointment confirmed'.

THE BIGGEST SECRET

The big secret is triggering a strong week by making a real estate sale on Monday morning. The bigger secret is having enough qualified buyers and motivated sellers in your pipeline to make that Monday sale possible.

The biggest secret of all: Keep your pipeline full.

It sounds simple – set appointments, study the market, make sales. And it is simple. It just isn't easy. But if you work with intention and intensity, you can absolutely do it.

Here is one promise I'll make to you: follow these guidelines consistently and you will find the sales performance and income you've been looking for. Now you know the secret. The only question is – what will you do with it?

Work Harder Than Ever to Achieve Success

Success doesn't come to those who wait for opportunities. It belongs to those who put in the effort. We live in a world full of distractions, and the temptation to take shortcuts is stronger than ever. But shortcuts lead to mediocrity.

If you want to succeed, you need to put in time, effort, and commitment. When others are resting, you're working. When others make excuses, you're finding solutions. When others wait for things to happen, you're creating your own opportunities. It's about going the extra mile when everyone else has given up.

Commit to working like you never have before. When others take time off, you keep pushing. If you want your goals to become reality, you have to go after them – don't expect them to come to you. Consistency is key.

Sacrifice is part of the journey. You may have to give up things others enjoy, like going to the beach or taking long breaks. Work like you never have before – the more you put in, the more you'll get out.

Commit fully to your goals. The rewards will come, but they come to those who work for them, day in and day out.

Hard work becomes a habit that shapes your future. Success belongs to those who never lose focus.

Real Estate Is Not a Job, It's a Lifestyle

Growing up, I never imagined I'd be in real estate. Back then, I thought work was just something you do to earn a living. I dreamed of a life where what you do doesn't feel like a job, it becomes part of who you are. That's exactly what real estate became for me when I got my full licence in 2010.

Let's be honest. Who wakes up saying, 'I want to sell homes, deal with people's problems, face rejection, and stay positive every single day?' Almost no one. Sales isn't glamorous. It's not easy. But real estate isn't just a career, it's personal transformation in action.

The top agents aren't just selling homes, they're shaping themselves. Real estate forces you to grow before it allows you to earn. It teaches resilience, patience, and discipline in ways most people never experience. High commissions aren't a reward, they're proof you can handle the pressure, uncertainty, and rejection that comes with this business.

You don't just learn how to sell – you learn how to lead conversations, guide outcomes, and regulate your emotions when rejection becomes routine. Real estate exposes your ego, your insecurities, and your excuses. Most people aren't willing to face themselves at that level. That's why so many quit early.

For me, real estate was never just about selling homes. It was about creating a lifestyle of growth, discipline, and mastery. By over-delivering for my clients, I built trust, earned referrals, and opened doors I never imagined. The money was a result – but the lifestyle, the personal transformation, and the freedom that came with it – that's the real reward.

Real estate is more than a job. It's a lifestyle that challenges you, pushes you, and rewards you in ways no traditional career ever could.

From Agent to Adviser

I introduce myself as a wealth creator for people in real estate or a property adviser. That's why, if you visit our website, **zedrealestate.com.au**, all our agents are titled Real Estate advisers. We guide clients from start to finish – A to Z. From renovation work to preparing a property for sale, hiring the right interior stylist, to selecting not just photographers but artisans so every photo in our marketing campaign tells a story – we manage it all.

We attract the right clientele and ensure they have the right finances. Our agents are knowledgeable about the cost of building materials, fixtures, and fittings so they don't just sell properties, they educate clients and explain why they should buy a home. When you explain the *why* to potential clients, the *how* becomes easy. It sounds professional, and people feel comfortable having a conversation with you. You're not just a real estate agent – you're running your own business within a business.

The secret to success in this field is to be persistent, consistent, and available whenever a client calls. After all, you're dealing with the biggest asset of their life. When the phone rings, you need to be ready to answer and ready to close the deal.

Leadership and Community Impact

As a real estate professional, you're not just a salesperson – you're a community leader. Whether you realise it or not, your actions, your visibility, and your service affect those around you. True leadership isn't just about being at the top – it's about being present, engaged, and valuable to your community.

Leadership doesn't always mean having a title. Sometimes it's as simple as being the person others ask for advice, or knowing your local area, or understanding what people need and connecting them to the right resources. Real estate is more than a career. It's a lifestyle, a platform, and a means to serve. That's what makes it so rewarding.

> "THE MOST SUCCESSFUL AGENTS AREN'T JUST THOSE WHO CLOSE THE MOST DEALS – THEY'RE THE ONES WHO LEAVE A LEGACY, BOTH IN BUSINESS AND IN THE HEARTS OF THEIR COMMUNITIES."

Never Quit

When you feel like quitting, remember why you started.

Real estate is the easiest job to get into and also the hardest job to survive in. Unlike other jobs, there is no salary or base wage, unless you're in the rental department or an executive assistant to one of the senior sales consultants. Life in sales is generally not fair. Some salespeople face more than their share of difficulties, while others close one big deal and get more breaks than they deserve. Nothing great comes from quitting. It's hard to be on your A-game every day, but keep going and think about what you're doing it all for. That's how Muhammad Ali became great. He even once said, 'I hated every minute of the training, but I said, Don't quit. Suffer now and live the rest of your life as a champion'.

"

NOTHING GREAT COMES
FROM QUITTING.

"

Don't Stop at Good Enough

Your greatest strength doesn't come from average effort. If you want average results, keep giving average effort. But if you want to be the best in your business, you must give your best – every single day.

Make a commitment to yourself that you won't leave the office until you've locked in four appointments for the day. Even if you fall short and land two, you're still ahead – because two is better than none.

I set this exact target for one of my team members. I told him, 'Minimum four appointments today.'

Later that evening, he called me and said, 'Zed, I think I'm done for the day. I've booked two.'

I said, 'You're not done yet. It's only 7:00 pm. You've got more to give.'

An hour later, he called me back and said, 'Thank God you pushed me. I just booked two more.'

That's when I told him, 'Now you can go home. Well done.'

The lesson is simple: most people stop too early. They settle the moment they get something, instead of pushing for what they're truly capable of.

Beat your daily goal. Beat your previous self. Break your own records.

No one else will do it for you.

"

IF YOU WANT TO BE THE BEST IN YOUR BUSINESS, GIVE YOUR BEST EFFORT.

"

HOW TO HIRE AND TRAIN TOP SALES PERFORMERS IN REAL ESTATE

When it comes to building a high-performing sales team, especially in real estate, hire individuals who have the right mindset, endurance, hunger to succeed, and the discipline to grow.

I hire people who have strong endurance. What I mean by that is this: if someone follows up with me multiple times for an interview, it shows they have the persistence to follow up with clients as well. It reflects how hungry and driven they truly are.

Whatever you see online – all the success and the number of properties being transacted – the truth is there's always a team involved behind every transaction. At Z. Real Estate, the word TEAM stands for *Together, Everyone Achieves More.*

Every billionaire got to where he or she is now by investing in personnel. So many companies claim to have had their start in a garage – Apple, Microsoft, Google, HP, and Amazon. Obviously, these industry titans are not run out of garages now, and one of the reasons for that is you can only fit so many people in a one-car bay.

You want growth? You want to be a billionaire like Jeff Bezos or Steve Wozniak? It takes a team.

The most successful agents aren't always the ones with the most experience – but the ones who are coachable, consistent, and carry themselves with professionalism every day.

An agency that stands out in a crowded marketplace, hires and trains top performers who don't just hit KPIs – they build careers, close deals, and grow your brand.

Attitude over Experience

Attitude isn't everything – but it's almost everything. A positive mindset, hunger to learn, and resilience in the face of rejection are far more valuable than ten years of average experience.

Having the right attitude always wins – and positivity breeds positivity. Clients can feel it, and it sets the tone for everything that follows.

Hire for attitude, train for skill. Look for people who ask questions, follow up, and aren't afraid to get uncomfortable. You can teach them the rest.

Product Knowledge is Power

You can't sell what you don't know. A real estate agent must know everything about their listings, market trends, zoning rules, and buyer behaviours. Being an expert makes you trustworthy – and people buy from people they trust.

Create a structured training plan. Each team member should know about the current listings in the area, core market data, comparable sales, objection handling answers, and construction basics

It's a good idea to run regular quizzes and role-plays. Repetition builds retention, which builds confidence.

Prospecting is the Skill that Pays

You can't rely on walk-ins or 'hot leads' forever. Great agents are great prospectors. They're not afraid to pick up the phone, knock on doors, or start conversations online.

Teach your team the art of prospecting. Set daily call targets, teach cold call scripts, and role-play objections. Make prospecting part of your culture – not a punishment, but a habit.

I'm great at listing properties because I'm a strong prospector. I embraced cold calling when others feared rejection or felt nervous on the phone. Instead of avoiding it, I leaned into it.

The more you prospect, the stronger you become. Every time someone hangs up on you, calls you names, or says no, you're building a muscle. You learn how to handle objections, stay composed, and keep moving forward. Over time, it becomes second nature.

That's why listing presentations becomes easy. When you've mastered prospecting, a listing presentation feels like a walk in the park. The confidence you build from cold calling or door knocking carries over into every conversation.

Embrace prospecting and watch what happens. You'll feel more confident, more in control, and more certain of your ability when you walk into any listing presentation.

It also changes how you think about money. You stop worrying about whether you can afford something or not. Instead, you tell yourself, *If I want it, I'll go make another call and get my next deal.*

Because at the end of the day, it's not money that makes money – it's the skill. And once you have the skill, you can always create more.

"

GREAT AGENTS ARE
GREAT PROSPECTORS.

"

Presentation Skills Make the Sale

You don't get a second chance at a first impression. The way an agent presents themselves – on the phone, at a listing appointment, or during a negotiation – sets the tone. Confidence, clarity, and connection are non-negotiables.

Keep your standards high and your coaching relentless. The ones who stick it out will become your next top performers.

STRATEGIES FOR SUCCESS IN REAL ESTATE: NAVIGATING MARKET SHIFTS, EMBRACING INNOVATION, AND BUILDING RESILIENCE

The landscape of the real estate market is continuously evolving, presenting both challenges and opportunities for professionals in the industry.

As I reflect on my journey in real estate, I recognise the significant changes that have taken place over the years. In the current scenario, a surge in economic prosperity has led to higher property prices, signalling a favourable market for sellers. However, this prosperity has also attracted a growing number of agents. More agents mean more competition in the industry. Regardless of the marketplace, agents who do well understand the market could shift at any time.

In my experience, I have witnessed a shift in perceptions regarding the value of properties, particularly in areas like Brighton that have undergone significant appreciation. Despite initial scepticism regarding property prices, I have always believed in the long-term growth potential of prime real estate. I have often advised buyers to consider the future value of their investments, emphasising the significance of acquiring properties in sought-after locations.

To prospective buyers, my counsel remains consistent: prioritise acquiring properties in prime locations, as the value of such investments typically appreciates over time. Invest in land as God doesn't make it anymore.

During periods of market downturn, sometimes it may be preferable to take a loss instead of holding onto that asset. The psychology of market sentiment plays a pivotal role in shaping transactions, as fear and uncertainty can deter potential buyers from capitalising on favourable opportunities.

In conclusion, thriving in the ever-changing real estate industry requires a combination of market awareness, adaptability, and a proactive mindset. By embracing innovation, maintaining a focus on long-term value, and cultivating resilience during challenging times, real estate professionals can position themselves for enduring success in a competitive marketplace.

“

SUCCESS IS SOMETHING YOU ATTRACT BY THE PERSON YOU BECOME. IT'S NOT SOMETHING YOU PURSUE; IT'S SOMETHING YOU DEVELOP.

”

The Key to Your Income: Philosophy and Discipline

Your income is directly related to your philosophy, not the economy or the marketplace. You need the discipline and processes to become the person you need to be. It's the skill that you learn over time that makes you the income as you could then apply it in all fields of life. Success is something you attract by the person you become. It's not something you pursue; it's something you develop.

Mastering the Art of Influence in Real Estate

1. Give a Nice Handshake and a Real Smile with Eye Contact

The client should break eye contact before you.

Your handshake conveys confidence and friendliness; it should be firm, but not bone-crushing, lasting two to five seconds. Practise your handshake with someone you trust and get feedback. Having a firm handshake is very attractive; it tells you a lot about your personality. And your smile should be so warm that it's beautiful.

2. Shine with Positivity

Before the meeting starts, act like it's already over and that you've won your client's business – humble yet confident at the same time. Immediately tell the person how great it is to see them, using their name. Nothing is sweeter to someone than the sound of their own name.

3. Take Control of the Conversation

As a real estate agent, understanding precisely what you want to achieve in every interaction is crucial. Whether it's showcasing a property to a potential buyer or negotiating a deal with a seller, having a clear agenda and direction can make all the difference. You must know precisely what you want from your interactions with others, and you must also know what you don't want.

4. Use the Competition to Brag About Yourself

Know your competitors' strengths and weaknesses and use them to your advantage. Suggest to potential clients that they should meet with other top salespeople. Sooner or later, most people will say, 'We need to see all our options'. The trick is to suggest the competition before anyone else does. It's about taking charge and showing confidence. It's the ultimate brag because it helps potential clients trust you as you're not perceived as being scared of the competition.

5. Respect All Players: Focus on Your Own Game

People won't want to work with agents who speak negatively about competitors. It's tacky, creates a negative cycle, and clients will be put off by a defensive nature. Choose instead to praise the competition, while including good points about your own business, such as, 'Competitor X is a really good company with a great platform. I would work for them if I hadn't chosen Z. Real Estate, which is the most followed real estate brand in the nation'. There was no need to mention Z. Real Estate making $200 million in sales. All I did was speak positively.

Yes, it's a tough game, but you can play tough and be professional and – most importantly – almost always win. Never bad-mouth the competition.

6. Lead with the Positives

There will always be positives and negatives about the product or service you're selling. I have a theory, which I practice when pitching, and it's my own take on the 80/20 rule. In the span of the pitch, I point out the positive 80 percent of the time and the negative 20 percent of the time. In mentioning the negatives, the positives are thereby reinforced, thereby gaining the trust of your clients.

Mastering Email Communication

There are many different theories on how to deal with email.

During my workday, I try to deal with emails in real-time for two reasons: Firstly, I love not having anything piling up. Secondly, it's very impressive for the person to hear back from you right away. It says that you're on your game. If you're answering in real-time, you'll find that you put out fires before they start and eliminate the need for storytelling and long explanations. I'd say nine out of ten of my emails can be answered in a line or two. Let me give you a few examples of my answers to emails from my day today:

Q: *Is this house available to be seen?*
A: Yes. Fred will be in touch to set it up. [cc'd my assistant in]

Q: *Do you have a property in the school zone with a swimming pool?*
A: Sure do, here is the link. It's in one of the best schools in the area.

Q: *Where do you want to eat tonight?*
A: Someplace healthy. You pick.

Q: *My client wants to pull out of the contract?*

A: All good no worries, I wish them all the best but call me please.

Mastering Time for Maximum Success

Your time on this planet is limited. Use it well. When I worked for LJ Hooker, I would walk into the office, say good morning from afar, and avoid small talk. There's nothing wrong with conversations between colleagues, but if you're focused on your goals, then stick to them and do justice to your time.

Don't let anyone steal your time. For me, when I'm not selling, I'm not making money – which means I'm actually losing money I could have been earning. If you don't serve clients, you don't pay the bills. Efficiency and time management are everything in this business.

"

DON'T LET ANYONE
STEAL YOUR TIME.

"

The Power of Honesty in Business and Real Estate

Honesty is incredibly important, especially in jobs like sales or service. Sometimes, people avoid telling the truth because they're afraid it could upset the customer or cause them to lose business. Homeowners always want quick feedback, and agents often feel pressure to keep them happy. However, lying or avoiding difficult truths won't help in the long run. Being honest is crucial in building trust and credibility. In a recent lawsuit, the person who told the truth won the case because his testimony was believable, unlike the one who contradicted himself by being dishonest.

If you tell the truth, you don't have to remember anything. Even if you think you might disappoint a client, it's always better to be honest, take responsibility for any mistakes, and work to make things right.

Work Smarter, Not Harder

I work hard but I don't stay busy for the sake of appearing busy. Everything I do is efficient and has an immediate and desired result.

One of my favourite quotes by Jim Rohn – you can tell he's had a big influence in my life and where I am today – 'Don't mistake movement with achievement. Just because you're in the office doesn't mean you're being dollar productive. Just because you're moving at work doesn't mean you're bringing value to the table'.

Just as researching homes for sale is an efficient use of time, so is giving yourself time to go for a walk, exercise, or spend time with your significant other and kids.

If you don't have something constructive right in front of you, look for it. Go through the motions of what you could be doing to create business. In the sales world, that might be hand-writing 60 notes and dropping them off in people's mailboxes or knocking on the doors of prospective clients to introduce yourself.

For me, timing is everything in life – whether you're closing a business deal, pursuing a new venture, or packing for a holiday. You have to get it done quickly and capably.

STANDING OUT IN REAL ESTATE SALES: BE A TRUSTED ADVISER, NOT A PUSHY SALESPERSON

Over the years, I've seen many salespeople use pushy tactics, pressuring people to buy without explaining *why* or highlighting the benefits of the product. I was raised in a household where my father told me, 'If you don't recommend something to yourself, don't recommend it to others.' Pushy tactics might work short-term, but they don't build lasting success. You see, customers don't pay you for what you do, they pay you for why you do it. Therefore, when you explain the why, the how becomes very easy.

Focus on building relationships by asking questions, understanding your clients' needs, and positioning yourself as an adviser rather than just a salesperson. Be the most informed and knowledgeable person in the room. Learn your product inside out, so when you get asked a question, you respond with confidence. This builds credibility and educates clients rather than simply closing a deal. Facts are always more convincing than emotions in sales.

If you know everything and everyone in your field, you'll likely do well. But if you choose not to, you're missing out. Knowledge builds confidence; ignorance builds fear.

> “
>
> FOCUS ON BUILDING RELATIONSHIPS BY ASKING QUESTIONS, UNDERSTANDING YOUR CLIENTS' NEEDS, AND POSITIONING YOURSELF AS AN ADVISER RATHER THAN JUST A SALESPERSON.
>
> ”

Be Fully Present with Your Clients

When you're with a client, be fully present. Put your phone away. If you can't, at least put it on silent. The last thing you want is your phone ringing in the middle of a negotiation. If you can't control it, get rid of the distraction completely. Never be on your phone while dealing with a client. It's rude and shows a lack of respect. I've seen salespeople check their phones in the middle of negotiations, and it's inexcusable. Focus on the moment and the person in front of you.

Listen More Than You Speak

There's a reason we have two ears and one mouth – we should listen twice as much as we speak. Clients often reveal everything you need to know without even realising it. You usually only get one chance to gather information, so make it count.

For example, after viewing a property in Brighton, I sat down with the seller to discuss working together. Before we talked about pricing, I asked a lot of questions. I wanted to understand them – what they care about, how they live, what's truly important. This information helped me serve them better. Instead of focusing on myself, I focused on listening and learning during that first conversation.

Ask Thoughtful Questions to Uncover Needs

During the visit, I noticed a beautiful piece of art in the foyer. I asked if they were art lovers – was it just a hobby or something more serious? Did they need more space for their collection? Were they looking for a home with plenty of natural light or maybe a studio? These subtle questions help me understand whether they're planning to buy another home while selling this one, without sounding pushy.

Pricing: A Collaborative Strategy

Once I have all the information, we move on to pricing. I know the prices of similar homes in the area but don't immediately share my opinion. Pricing a home is like a game – I start by asking sellers what they hope to achieve. Often, they say, 'That's why you're here'. Then I ask if they've had other agents out and what those agents recommended regarding price and selling methods.

I want to hear their experience before I offer my opinion. I use this to read my vendors and ask about their previous sales experiences – whether they sold privately or via auction and how that worked out. If they had an unsuccessful auction or didn't like it, I recommend a private sale. If they used private sale before, I'd suggest an auction. These questions help me understand their preferences so I can suggest a fair price and strategy without risking the listing.

By being a trusted adviser – fully present, deeply knowledgeable, and genuinely interested – you'll outshine your competition every time.

Knowledge is Key in Real Estate! Mastering Market Details for Success

Knowing the market is the smartest way to show value as an agent. Clients will trust and listen to you for the important details.

High-end property clients are smart – they usually run their own businesses, manage global accounts, or have some sort of influence in the world. They pay attention to details and won't tolerate nonsense or what I call the sales spell. Take off your salesman hat and become more of an adviser, add value, and educate. Don't be pushy. However, they don't always choose a home based on rational factors, so it's crucial you know your stuff, paying attention to both the logical and emotional factors at play. That's how you provide your clients with a unique experience.

Know Your Stuff

While you can stand out from your colleagues by being the most polished, professional, and proactive, if you're not also the most knowledgeable about your product, your presentation, your service, your cause, none of the above matters. In my business, knowing my stuff means that I practically know everything about the market, and I have the thirst to learn more. I can't relax because the marketplace is always changing. Real estate news is always in flux. If a house sells above or below reserve, I'll find out why. If a good property at a reasonable price isn't moving, I'll get the details. My business thrives on information, so my ear is always to the ground. This helps me stand out from the competition.

SUCCESS IS BUILT ON STRUCTURE: ACTIONS AND HABITS THAT DRIVE RESULTS

Success is built on structure and habits. There are no shortcuts. Here are some proven habits and strategies to help sharpen your skills and build maximum success.

Track Time with Intention

Maintain an accurate diary for 14 days. Document *everything* – from phone calls and meetings to admin work and breaks. Be honest. Track how many real conversations (connects) you're having versus how many attempts (non-connects). This simple habit will give you visibility into where your time is really going and how you can improve your efficiency.

"

SUCCESS IS BUILT ON STRUCTURE AND HABITS. THERE ARE NO SHORTCUTS.

"

Master the Art of Prospecting Calls

Learn how to make effective prospecting calls – *and do them consistently*. Track the time and frequency of your calls, and aim for a minimum of 200 connections per week. But remember: don't mistake movement for achievement. It's not just about how many calls you make – it's about the quality and outcome of each interaction. Stay intentional and focused.

Clear the Clutter and Create Focus

Your desk reflects your mindset. Clear off anything unnecessary. Keep only what you need in front of you and remove distractions. If it helps, place a printed list of your short-term and long-term goals – maybe even with images – on your desk or set it as your desktop background. That way, every time you sit down, you're reminded of why you're doing this.

Block Your Time Like a Pro

High performers don't 'wing it' – they time-block. Structure your day by allocating specific time slots for:

- Buyer call-backs
- Prospecting potential vendors
- Follow-ups with current vendors
- Appraisals and listing presentations
- Submitting properties to qualified buyers
- Mid-campaign check-ins and pre-auction strategy meetings
- Market research and competitor analysis

When each task has a set time, your days become more productive and less reactive. You'll find yourself getting more done, in less time – with better results.

Eliminate Low-Value Tasks

Stop wasting your precious time on low-value tasks. Your time is best focussed on sales. Here are some surefire ways to eliminate unnecessary tasks and stay laser-focussed on sales.

Outsource Copywriting

Use a professional copywriter to write property ads. At Z, our in-house operations team works around the clock to handle ad copy and content which frees agents to focus on high-value tasks.

Don't Attend Property Photoshoots

Let your photographer do their job. Set clear expectations, then step aside. If they aren't delivering, find someone who will. Your time is better spent on income-generating activities.

Avoid Getting Caught Up in Building/Pest Inspections

Delegate where possible. These aren't dollar-productive tasks. Let your assistant handle them while you focus on your next listing or closing.

> "
>
> WHEN EACH TASK HAS A SET TIME,
> YOUR DAYS BECOME MORE
> PRODUCTIVE AND LESS REACTIVE.
>
> "

Sell Smarter, Not Harder

It's all about strategy. When you're driven to sell smarter, you focus on knowing your customer, targeting the right opportunities, and implementing tools that help you achieve your goal. To sell without strategy is hard work, it's like a hamster on a wheel, endlessly spinning without any impact.

I've outlined below some of the methods I've used that have propelled me to sell smarter, not harder.

Meet Both Decision-Makers

Have both parties present at an appraisal. That way, you avoid objections like, 'Let me speak to my partner' and can close the deal.

Pre-Qualify Buyers Before Private Inspections

Don't waste time. Confirm finance is ready, and ensure all decision-makers will be present. One solid inspection is better than three half-hearted ones. If a buyer is vague, move on.

Direct Buyers to OFIs When Possible

Be selective with what properties you show. Ask the right questions to filter buyers properly. Don't show a townhouse to a family clearly after a backyard. Educate them on what's realistic in their price range.

Qualify OFI Buyers Properly

Build rapport. They buy *you* before they buy the house. Every buyer could be a future vendor – leave a lasting positive impression.

Cut Off Time-Wasters

If a buyer is unrealistic or unqualified, smile and move on. Don't let them eat up your month while you chase a ghost sale.

Be Ruthlessly Efficient

Wasting time looks harmless enough, but every moment spent on empty distractions is a moment stolen from the things that matter in your life. Your business, definitely. Your creativity and family. Being ruthlessly efficient is not about being endlessly productive; it's about recognising that your time is precious. When you give it away to things that don't matter, you're essentially trading pieces of your future for nothing in return.

Prioritise the Right Tasks

Start each day with intention. Know your goals. Avoid distractions. Focus only on the work that moves the needle.

Start the Day Fast

Slow starts kill productivity. Come in ready to go. A fast start sets the tone for a successful day.

Keep Breaks Short and Sharp

Stay locked in. You can relax after hours – work time is for working.

Stay Organised

Be structured, tidy, and keep your systems tight.

"

BEING RUTHLESSLY EFFICIENT IS NOT ABOUT BEING ENDLESSLY PRODUCTIVE; IT'S ABOUT RECOGNISING THAT YOUR TIME IS PRECIOUS.

"

Be the CEO of Your Time

Your time is your most valuable currency. Spend it wisely. Cut the fluff. Maximise output. Operate like a businessperson, not just an agent. Build your days around habits that generate income and build momentum.

In this industry, you don't rise to the level of your goals – you fall to the level of your systems.

So build the right ones.

SUCCESS IN REAL ESTATE: ADAPTING, EVOLVING, AND GROWING

Success in real estate means being smart and flexible as the market changes. To do well, agents need to be quick to adjust to new trends and come up with fresh ideas. The best agents keep up with what's happening in the industry and continuously improve how they work to give clients what they need.

In some areas, like Brighton, house prices have increased exponentially. Even when others doubted the value of buying there, I always believed it was a good long-term move. I tell buyers to think ahead and invest in places that will likely go up in value over time.

When the market is down, many people hesitate to buy because they're worried. Everyone comes out with their convertible cars when the sun is shining and nobody brings them out when it's raining. History shows that real estate markets can bounce back. Emotions, like fear, can stop buyers from making smart choices when there are good deals to be had.

During tough times like the COVID lockdown, I implemented new ideas and technology to stay in touch with clients and keep property deals going. Adapting to changes and finding chances for growth in hard times is key to doing well in real estate. By always getting better, learning new things, and getting ready for surprises in the market, agents can keep their business strong.

To succeed in real estate, it's vital to be aware of market changes, be ready to adapt, and have a proactive outlook. By being open to new ideas, focusing on long-term gains, and staying strong in tough times, real estate pros can set themselves up for enduring success in a competitive field.

THE POWER OF ONE: WHY EVERY HIGH PERFORMER NEEDS A TRUE EQUAL

On the journey to success, there's one relationship that can make all the difference – not a mentor, not a follower, but an **equal**.

An equal walks beside you – not ahead, not behind. They're more than a friend, and definitely not a yes-person. They're a trusted confidant who challenges your thinking, questions your assumptions, and supports your growth – both personally and professionally.

They're the one person you can be completely real with. No filters. No ego. Just raw honesty, mutual respect, and a shared desire to see each other win.

An equal tells you the truth, even when it's uncomfortable. They'll call you out when you're off track and push you when you start to coast. And when you succeed? They'll be your loudest cheerleader.

With an equal, you can feel comfortable exchanging ideas without judgement, debating without ego, failing without fear, and – perhaps the best of all – laughing without pretending.

For me, that person is Amir; my best friend, who is formally educated in the finance world and is like a god of finance. Every time he talks, his point is sincere and comes from a place of credentials and honesty. He never lets me settle. He challenges my boldest ideas, questions my logic, and keeps my ambition in check with discipline.

Through our deep conversations and honest feedback, I've grown more than I ever could from any course or book. He's helped me sharpen my thinking, strengthen my focus, and elevate how I operate – not just in business, but in life.

LEARN TO SAY NO: MASTERING THE ART OF BOUNDARIES IN REAL ESTATE

When you're starting out in real estate, it's easy to say yes to everything. Every listing, every buyer, every request. In the early stages, it's all about the numbers game – the more people you speak to, the more doors you knock on, the more opportunities you create. And that's the truth.

At that stage, volume equals momentum. You build experience, grow your network, and create brand recognition through sheer hustle. You take the difficult listings, the unrealistic vendors, the time-wasters – because any listing is better than no listing.

But as you grow, things change. You start to realise that not all business is good business.

Now, I believe there's nothing worse than working with people who drain your energy or bring toxic energy to the table. I'm at a stage in my career where if it doesn't feel right – I walk away. I now understand the value of my time, energy, and mental clarity. Time is the most valuable asset – and no amount of commission can buy it back.

"

TIME IS THE MOST VALUABLE ASSET – AND NO AMOUNT OF COMMISSION CAN BUY IT BACK.

"

NEGOTIATION

An essential aspect of being a successful dealmaker is understanding the buyer's perspective. If a client feels pressured, they are likely to put up their guard and question your credibility as a trusted adviser.

To transition from a sales-centric approach to deal-making, it's crucial to have a clear opinion. Offering informed guidance and adding value to the client's decision-making process is key. While some salespeople may just agree with everything a client says to avoid conflict, authentic dealmakers provide honest and insightful opinions based on their expertise.

As an agent, it's vital to educate clients about the market and provide them with information to make informed decisions. Trust is built through honesty and transparency, even if it means steering clients away from properties that may not be the best fit.

Deal-makers prioritise their clients' best interests above all else. Instead of focusing on short-term sales, they aim to build long-term relationships with repeat buyers by guiding them towards wise investments and protecting them from potential pitfalls.

In real estate, being a dealmaker means being a knowledgeable and trustworthy guide for clients. It involves having a deep understanding of the market and property details, and prioritising the client's well-being over quick sales.

So, are you a salesperson or a dealmaker? If you aspire to be a dealmaker, your clients will appreciate the value and integrity you bring to the table.

One of the smartest moves you can make as a dealmaker is to increase your social circle; for me, the more people I know, the more potential clients I have. As a social animal, it's my nature to make friends, so this is just an added benefit to being a dealmaker. I love talking to new people! Sometimes I drive my friends and family crazy when we're out together and I spend so much time chatting with everyone around us. There's never a stranger when I'm nearby.

Cultivating relationships is not only pleasant and entertaining, but it's a sure way to enhance your business. I do favours for friends all the time, and they react in kind.

Because of the relationships I've since fostered, I have a myriad of folks I can rely on to have my back, and I have theirs too. I can dole out assistance to or call it in from people everywhere, anywhere from A to Z. I have built my network and relationships with people in every industry.

NEGOTIATE HIGH-END DEALS WITH CONFIDENCE

To negotiate truly high-end deals, having confidence is not enough; you must put yourself into a millionaire's shoes.

If you come at every deal like you're a millionaire, you won't be too intimidated to fight for what you need. A real millionaire would never get hung up on the small stuff that's taken to get them there, such as advertising and marketing costs, or the expense of paying for a team; so you shouldn't, either. The saying, 'You must spend money to make money', holds true.

Remember this – a millionaire who's selling their $5 million home doesn't care whether they make the deal or not. So the only way to get that contract signed and squeeze every penny out of it is to react in kind and pretend that you, another millionaire, have nothing to lose either.

FIVE PRINCIPLES OF NEGOTIATION: HOW TO WIN WITHOUT FORCING IT

Negotiation isn't about pressure – it's about **control, awareness, and understanding people**. The best negotiators don't fight harder; they think smarter.

1. Understand the Person, Not Just the Deal

Negotiation is not about numbers, it's about people.

Before you even step into a conversation, do your homework. Learn who you're dealing with. Look at their background, their behaviour, and their personality. When you meet them, observe everything, including their tone, body language, eye contact, and reactions.

Ask yourself: Are they driven by logic… or ego?

Some people care more about *feeling like they've won* than the actual outcome. If that's the case, let them feel heard. Let them feel in control. Ask questions like: 'What would you do if you were in my position?' Now they're opening up, sharing their thoughts and giving you insight into how to close the deal. If they're inexperienced, guide them. Build trust. Speak like a partner, not a salesperson: 'We're in this together'.

When people trust you, they stop resisting you.

2. Acknowledge Before You Influence

People don't want to be argued with, they want to be understood.

Match their energy. If they're calm, be calm. If they're direct, be direct. This creates comfort and connection.

One of the simplest but most powerful tools is this: **Repeat their points back to them.** It shows you're listening. It lowers their guard. It builds trust. Negotiation isn't a battle. It's a conversation. When people feel heard, they become open to new ideas. That's when you can guide the conversation towards a solution that works for both sides.

3. Don't Chase Yes – Create Better Questions

Most people negotiate the wrong way. They push for a 'yes'. But yes doesn't always mean commitment. And no doesn't always mean rejection.

Instead of asking 'Can you meet tomorrow?', ask 'Does 10 or 4 work better for you?' Now they're choosing, not rejecting.

A better question creates a better outcome. Try this, 'Would it be unreasonable to ask for a higher offer?' Now you've opened a real discussion.

The goal isn't to force agreement. It's to **move the conversation forward**.

4. Use Silence as a Strategy

Most people talk too much in negotiations – and that's where they lose. Silence is power.

When you stop talking, the other person starts thinking. And when they start thinking, they often start solving the problem for you. Silence creates space. Space creates clarity. Clarity creates decisions.

Let them speak first. Then respond with intention.

5. Stay Calm When It Matters Most

Anyone can stay positive when things are easy. The real test is when things get difficult. The moment emotions take over, the deal starts to fall apart. Stay calm. Stay patient. Stay in control.

I once closed a $9 million deal where the client wanted full control and constantly interrupted. The deal nearly collapsed multiple times.

The only reason it worked? I stayed calm, I listened more than I spoke and I kept the energy positive, even when it was frustrating. That's what got it across the line.

Remind your clients, 'We're in this together. I'm on your side'. When people feel that, they stay in the deal.

Remember:

Negotiation is a skill and like any skill, it needs to be trained. The more you practise, the stronger you become. Because in the end, you're not just closing deals, you're mastering people.

LEARN FAST, DON'T REPEAT MISTAKES

It's fine to make mistakes, but if it becomes a pattern, reflect on what you're overlooking and how to avoid it in the future. Practice the basics to prevent repeating those mistakes. And remember, sometimes saying no is the best option.

I don't care what stage of your career you're in, you're going to make mistakes. They're unavoidable. The goal is that you use the experience to strengthen yourself as a dealmaker. At the very least, the hope is you don't keep doing the same thing wrong over and over, because that's just sloppy.

Don't be sloppy.

If you want to up your attitude, start to self-reflect. Look back on where you've been professionally and make an honest assessment. You won't be able to strengthen your weak spots until you determine what they are.

I went into my career with the attitude that failure was not an option... except it totally was. If I didn't make it as a real estate agent, I wasn't going to be homeless or hungry. My family was an impenetrable safety net, but I neither recognised, acknowledged, nor appreciated this fact. You know the expression, 'What would you do if you knew you couldn't fail?' That sums up my life, except I had no clue as I'd never experienced anything else. I still worked like my safety and security depended on it, and I expected the kudos for when it worked out exactly like I'd planned. Let me say this – it's a hell of a lot easier to get to home plate when you're starting on third base.

CONFIDENCE IS CONTAGIOUS

The truth is, no matter how good you are at something in life, you always need to push yourself past your limits. If you expect to get small clients, you'll get small clients. Confidence is something your buyer can sniff out from a mile away. How can you expect someone you work with to trust you with their sale if you don't trust your own abilities?

The key to understanding my attitude is that I am never not Zelling an image and a lifestyle. This is a constant in my life.

I know how to get into any door. Again, it all boils down to confidence.

We're suspicious of the person who enters a place and projects anxiety, like they're about to be caught. Nervous, fidgeting – they're all dead giveaways that person doesn't belong. But no one stops the guy or gal who strides in like he or she owns the place.

The best advice is to always act like you've been there before, even if you haven't, regardless of the circumstance.

Let me clue you in on what makes or breaks an effective deal-maker – the absolute belief that your product, service, or idea will improve the buyer's life or circumstances. (This is far easier if you follow my advice and sell something for which you're passionate.) Naturally, you want to make the deal because you'll get a cheque, which goes without saying. But if you look at a sale as the most expedient way to pay your bills and that's it, you're not set up for long-term success.

In my job, I'm confident in approaching people because I'm certain that they'll be happier when selling their home, or the improved quality of life they'll experience after buying one. (Remember, I don't sell garbage, and this is yet another reason why.)

I see myself as an adviser on improving my clients' lives. Think of it like this – if you knew how much better people would sleep at night having bought from you, wouldn't you feel incredible about yourself?

Wouldn't you be fearless in approaching potential customers, excited even, secure in the knowledge that you can exponentially increase their contentment by solving a problem they didn't even know they had? This mindset applies to any deal you might make, in any industry.

Assess the product, service, or idea you hope to zell. Look beyond the features and benefits – what are the advantages?

Use those advantages to build your confidence in your product and yourself.

For example, say you're Zelling a chef's knife. The feature is that the blade is thin, and the benefit is that the blade size makes it ideal for more precise tasks, like slicing chicken for salad.

The advantage is that a thin, hard blade means less sharpening, which not only saves time but also helps prevent the kind of accidents that stem from a dull knife; and no chef wants to tend to an injury in the middle of a dinner shift.

Suddenly, you're not pushing knives, you're protecting livelihoods.

And doesn't that feel great?

> “NEVER TAKE THE FIRST OFFER. THEY'RE NOT FINAL. THEY'RE NOT THE BEST. THEY'RE NOT SACRED.”

DON'T SWEAT THE SMALL STUFF

Regardless of how clear the path from A to Z may seem, encountering roadblocks is inevitable on the way to closing a deal. How you handle small problems directly affects how others perceive your ability to manage the larger ones.

Create strategies for navigating around or capitalising on anything that feels like a problem, because it might just be a solution in disguise. Anything you encounter, whether it's a shift in the market or a challenge to your reputation, can be handled when you make the decision to not sweat the small stuff.

Sometimes, taking a step back for perspective reveals that even the most daunting challenges are, in fact, 'small stuff'.

The First Offer is Just the Beginning: Hold Out for More

If there's one rule in real estate that will never fail you, it's this: Never take the first offer. They're not final. They're not the best. They're not sacred.

Jumping at the first offer screams desperation – and desperation is the fastest way to lose control in a negotiation.

The first offer is the opening move in a game of chess. It's a buyer saying, 'Let's see if they bite'. Don't bite. Even when there's only one offer on the table, your job is to act like it's just one of many. You hold the cards. You set the tone. You control the pace. Confidence = leverage. And leverage is everything.

Use Perception to Your Advantage

Here's the truth: most buyers are unsure of how much power they really have. So, if you can maintain composure, create a little uncertainty, and look like you're in control, they'll assume you are – and they'll pay more just to feel like they're still in the game.

Imagine this: You receive an offer on a listing. It's decent, but you know there's more room to move.

Instead of calling your client to celebrate, you say, 'We've got interest – this is just the start. Let's see how far we can push this'.

Then, you go back to the buyer and say, 'Appreciate the offer. We've had strong interest – my vendor is reviewing all serious options, but you're in the mix. If you want to strengthen your position, now's the time'.

Boom. Pressure applied.

Negotiation is a Performance

You don't need ten buyers to create urgency. You need to act like the deal isn't done yet.

Remember: buyers are emotional. They don't want to lose. FOMO (fear of missing out) is a powerful tool in negotiation.

Your job as the agent is to create tension, hold your ground, use silence, timing and confidence.

There's Always Another Deal

One of the biggest mistakes agents make is working from fear. *What if this is the only offer we get? What if they walk away?*

Here's your new mindset: If they walk, someone else will come. And if they don't, it wasn't your deal. The right one is around the corner. You're not in this game to scrape by – you're in it to dominate.

Key Takeaways

- Don't accept the first offer. It's never the best one.
- Create controlled tension. Use psychology to your advantage.
- Keep your client calm. Remind them that patience = profit.
- Negotiate like a pro. Talk less. Say more. Move with purpose.
- Know when to walk away. You can't lose what wasn't right for you.

Understand Behaviour. Control the Deal.

Every great negotiator – whether they know it or not – is a student of human behaviour. They don't manipulate with pressure; they guide decisions by understanding what drives people to act.

Here's the key: People hate being told what to do. But they love doing things when they think it was their idea.

Psychology, Not Pressure

Let me give it to you straight: if you want to influence clients, buyers, sellers – anyone – you need to speak to their emotions, not just their logic. That means applying empathy over ego, suggestions over commands, and compliments over criticism.

Real persuasion is like a chess game. You're thinking five moves ahead – not because you're trying to win over your client, but because you're trying to help them win without ever realising you guided them there.

Real Estate Example: The Ugly Gold Chair

Let's say a seller has an awful gold chair with pink cushions sitting proudly in the living room. It's an eyesore. You know it. Every buyer will know it.

But here's what I won't say, 'That chair is terrible. You need to get rid of it.'

Instead, I'll say, 'You and I have such similar taste – refined and sophisticated. Not everyone will appreciate our level of style, though. If we neutralise the space just a little, we'll appeal to a wider audience.'

Now, the seller feels seen, appreciated, and empowered – not criticised.

Still, let's say they ignore the advice. A few weeks pass, and no offers come through. Here's what I'll say next, 'I've been thinking about what you said in that meeting. You were spot on. I actually think your idea of removing those personal items could really help us re-engage buyers.'

Boom. They feel like a genius, and the chair is gone.

Plant the Seed. Let It Grow.

If you want long-term success in any sales-based business, learn this: People rarely listen to experts. But they always follow their own ideas.

So make your idea feel like their idea. That's the real art of persuasion. It's not about being right.

It's about being smart enough to get what's right done, without making it about your ego.

Key Persuasion Tactics You Can Use Today:

- **Use praise to position advice.** 'You've got great instincts. Here's a tweak I think we should consider together.'
- **Create emotional distance.** 'Let's look at this home through a buyer's eyes. What would they want to see?'
- **Delay and redirect.** If they resist at first, wait. Circle back later with their 'own' idea.
- **Play the long game.** Don't push hard and lose rapport. Nudge gently and win influence over time.

The best persuaders don't shout. They whisper. They don't demand. They suggest. They don't say, 'I told you so'. They say, 'You were right all along'.

If you want to master the art of Zelling, stop trying to sell people – and start helping them decide.

That's persuasion done right.

THE ART OF FACE-TO-FACE NEGOTIATION

If any deal or life situation isn't going the way you'd like, the best damage control you can do is get in a room with the person and talk it out. This might not always be possible, but if it is, make it happen. If you've been communicating with someone through email and your price isn't being accepted, the contract isn't getting signed, or negotiations are turning sour, immediately ask to meet face-to-face. Write 'CALL ME!' in the subject line and nothing else. That's how to get the other party's attention. When they call, say, 'We need to meet. I'm coming over. I'll be there in ten'.

In today's society, where all of us have our brains connected to our phones and emails all day long, this is often easier said than done. But try to make it happen.

More than 70 percent of our communication is expressed without words – yes, that's right! Seventy percent! A great negotiator uses emotions, family heritage, spirituality, body language, fashion, sexuality (oh yes!), humour, and everything else in between to win and make a deal happen. How can you ever use those skill sets in an email? Your emotions, excitement, and mood are all communicated through your body. No number of emojis or exclamation marks can make up for that.

Also, it's much more difficult to say no to someone sitting in front of you, but very easy to type 'No' in an email or avoid someone's phone call. When the phone is your only option, always have an agenda. Know what you want out of the phone call before making it. Keep the calls short. The best phone negotiators use few words, where every word is important and meaningful. Speak clearly and with weight. Rid yourself of verbal tics. When someone says 'uh' and 'you know' repeatedly in any conversation, it makes me cringe. If it's during a negotiation, it puts that person in the awkward position of sounding dumb or insecure. Pause between your counterpart's talking and your response. Speak like it's final, without question marks.

And please, don't negotiate on the phone outside on a windy street next to a construction site. Nothing irritates someone more than having to repeat something five times because you can't hear them.

Negotiation Theatre: How to Control the Room and Close the Deal

Negotiation is a game of opposites. When things start looking predictable... you've already lost the upper hand.

The truth? Great negotiators are great actors. You have to be ready to perform, pivot, bluff, and play – because the biggest wins come to those who aren't afraid to shake things up.

Predictability Kills Power

When your opponent knows exactly what to expect from you, they're already preparing their countermove. But when you control the tempo – when you surprise them – you create emotional uncertainty. And *that's* where the leverage lives.

Let me walk you through one of my personal favourite techniques – what I call the 'emotional curveball'.

1. **Start High** – I walk into a negotiation warm, smiling, confident, charismatic. I'll give a hug, crack a joke, or even say, 'I love you already – this deal's going to be easy.' They drop their guard. They think, 'This guy's a softie. I've got this.'
2. **Drop Low** – Then, I suddenly shift gears. I say, 'Look, to be honest… I don't think this is going to work.' I've caught them off guard. The room shifts. Now *they* feel like they might lose something.
3. **Let It Burn** – I let the tension rise. I go quiet. Maybe I look disappointed or even a little frustrated. I lean back and say something like, 'I thought we had alignment, but clearly not. I'm not sure this is worth pushing.' This is the **emotional low point**. And now they're trying to save the deal.
4. **Bring Back Hope** – Once they're leaning in, I toss them a little lifeline, 'Maybe… if we can tweak just one thing, we could make it work.' Hope is electric. Their minds are racing. They're back in the game – but this time, **on your terms**.
5. **Close Strong** – I end on a high note, rebuild the energy, and *drive it home*. The result is a closed deal, a price elevated, and everyone walking away feeling like they won – even if you controlled the whole dance.

People buy and negotiate based on emotion first, logic second. Think about it. You can't see the power of light unless you've been in the dark. You can't appreciate peace until there's been tension. You can't negotiate like a boss if you keep everything flat and predictable.

Emotions *amplify* perception.

If you can guide the emotional rhythm of a negotiation – highs and lows, tension and release – you'll lead the entire show.

Negotiation isn't just numbers on a spreadsheet – it's psychology, emotion, and theatre. If you want to win, make sure you know your lines. Read the room. And never, ever let them know your next move.

Let them feel the sunshine, then let it rain, then bring back the light. Because when you control the storm, you control the deal.

"

NEGOTIATION ISN'T JUST NUMBERS ON A SPREADSHEET – IT'S PSYCHOLOGY, EMOTION, AND THEATRE.

"

THE POWER OF BODY LANGUAGE IN NEGOTIATION

When you're in a room with someone discussing something important, remember that you're communicating not only with your words but also with your body. It's crucial that both are in alignment. If you want someone to meet your demands, keep your arms open, smile, and sit closer.

Conversely, if you're dissatisfied with the terms or situation, cross your arms and sit further away.

I realised by the time I graduated from Dandenong High School that body language tells a story, and sometimes, our faces reveal everything. You are in control of a conversation when you're smiling sincerely and maintaining eye contact. However, when you begin to look away, squint, bite your lip, or clench your jaw, you're signalling that things aren't going the way you want. This is fine, if your intention is to let the other party know you find their offer unacceptable or their terms unrealistic.

Most people haven't watched themselves negotiate, so they may not even realise they are sending these signals. When I talk with people, I try to keep my arms and hands relaxed, often resting them in my lap. I almost never cross my arms, and I would only clench my fists if my hands are hidden under the table. When I used to bite my nails, the worst was getting caught doing so while negotiating – it essentially shouted to the other side that they were getting to me. Remember, negotiating is like poker. Never let the other side know what your next move will be – don't allow your face to reveal your cards.

Be mindful of your legs and feet as well. Stop shaking your legs or tapping your feet under the table. If I'm standing up during a negotiation, I open my suit jacket and lean in towards the person I'm talking to, focusing my energy on their face.

I sometimes zigzag between two extremes to create a bit of confusion intentionally. This tactic takes practice, but it works well for me. I might say something like 'This offer sucks', with a cute and boyish demeanour. By doing this, the negative information is more easily absorbed, like dressing up the bad news in a less intimidating way. It signals that I'm unhappy but open to continuing the conversation.

I love reading the other person's body language during negotiations because it reveals so much. Pay attention to their subtle 'tells' – small giveaways that show what they're thinking. For example, if someone is trying to act tough and in control, refusing to budge on their offer, you might notice their jaw clenching or their foot tapping. If they were truly comfortable with their position, they'd be more relaxed. Or if they're at their highest limit, you might notice them looking resigned, slowly acknowledging that the deal isn't going to happen.

NEGOTIATION RULES

Negotiation is a skill that's refined over time through practice, observation, and experience. Your success as a real estate agent hinges on your ability to negotiate effectively, while always maintaining professionalism, respect, and care for all parties involved. Objections arise because the person you're speaking with hasn't fully received your message the way you intended.

When selling, focus on identifying and selling the value of what you're offering. Solve the customer's problem, and ask for the payment. There's no need for negotiation if you've successfully communicated the value. Negotiate only when absolutely necessary.

It's natural to lose a bit of confidence when entering a negotiation. Thoughts like, *How much can I get away with?* or, *What's the right offer?* might come to mind. The key is to stop negotiating with yourself. Don't second-guess your value or your offer. Never negotiate out of fear, but never fear to negotiate. Stand firm in your value and don't undercut yourself before you even start.

The Silent Advantage: Why Listening Wins More Deals Than Talking Ever Will

Great negotiators listen twice as much as they speak. In a world full of noise, interruptions, and people talking just to hear themselves – true listening is rare. And powerful.

Most people are waiting for their turn to talk. Top negotiators listen in the same way hawks watch: waiting, absorbing. When you truly listen, you uncover important messages, including what the other side really wants (even if they don't say it outright), the emotional drivers behind their decisions, and their motivations, and pressure points.

This is your ammunition. Every word they speak gives you a clearer roadmap to close the deal.

Real Estate Example: Read Between the Lines

Seller: 'I just want to get this done quickly.'

If you're listening with intent, you'll hear more than just speed. You'll hear urgency, possible financial pressure, and maybe emotional fatigue.

That's when I might say, 'Totally understand – timing is everything. If we price this right and present it beautifully, I can generate serious interest in the first seven days. That way, we don't just get it sold fast, we get it ZOLD right.'

Now you're not just responding. You're solving.

The Power of the Pause

Silence makes people uncomfortable – but it also makes them speak. Try this: Next time you're negotiating, ask a question… then pause.

Stay quiet.

You'll be surprised how much more the other person reveals when you don't rush to fill the silence.

That quiet moment? It's where the truth slips out.

The Ultimate Negotiation Formula

To master negotiation – and truly build trust – you need to know:

1. When to speak – Deliver value, clarity, and confidence.
2. When to listen – Uncover hidden details and emotional drivers.
3. When to stand firm – Back yourself and your value, no matter what.

Listening isn't passive – it's an active power move. While everyone else is busy pitching, talking, convincing, and overexplaining, you're the one in control – gathering insights, building trust, and setting yourself up for a strategic, persuasive win. Want to be unforgettable in any negotiation?

Talk less. Listen more. Win bigger.

"

WANT TO BE UNFORGETTABLE IN ANY NEGOTIATION? TALK LESS. LISTEN MORE. WIN BIGGER.

"

BRANDING

PROMOTE YOURSELF AND YOUR BRAND

'It takes twenty years to build a reputation and five minutes to ruin it. If you think about that, you'll do things differently.'

Warren Buffett, chairman and CEO of Berkshire Hathaway

Your Email Address Reflects Your Brand

Please never use a Gmail, Yahoo, or Hotmail email address for professional purposes. Not having a properly branded email address is a huge red flag that you are not taking your brand seriously. It is important to own your personal domain and establish an email address associated with that domain name. This goes beyond branding; it's about presenting the most polished, professional version of yourself at every step of the client-customer interaction. Sure, free email domains are fine for personal correspondence, but using your own domain adds a level of security and professionalism that will help you stand out from the crowd.

Here is an example of using my name: zed@zedrealestate.com.au This email address is easily connected to me, and it's easy to remember and share.

UNCOVER YOUR BRAND IDENTITY

How Do You See Yourself?

At this very moment, take time to reflect on who you are. Set a timer for twenty minutes, and during that time, jot down as many adjectives as you can that describe YOU. Be bold and confident – there's no need to hold back or over-analyse. Just create a comprehensive list of words that capture who you truly are and what you stand for.

How Do Others See You?

You got the ball rolling with that first exercise – the next will focus on how you are viewed by others.

- How would clients describe you?
- Why would clients refer you to other people?

Collect any client testimonials in one place. Get out your pen and go to work, highlighting any adjectives that have been used to describe you. If you're willing to take this process further, you can! Send a text to your colleagues or clients you've worked with and ask, "How would you describe me in five words?"

Reconcile and Refine

Locate the Zone of Authenticity.

The words you've written down that correlate with each other are your zone of authenticity. It's that sweet spot where what you think and what people think of you meet.

THIS IS WHO YOU ARE!

These words are the best potential candidates for your power adjectives.

Test out those power adjectives. Write down the three power adjectives you've curated from the steps above. You might be over the moon about what you've discovered. You've nailed it! Or maybe you're feeling, 'Wait, am I really edgy, innovative, and perceptive?'

Remember, while power adjectives are IMPORTANT, there are no right or wrong answers here. Ultimately, this is about what feels right to you. It's about which words motivate you to get wildly excited about taking your brand to the next level. There is no rule that says people who sell high-end real estate need to be polished – that's my authentic take on my brand. What works for you doesn't necessarily work for other people. These words are impacted by your take on them, and there are many valid ways to find adjectives to describe your brand personality.

Now that you have completed this exercise, you should fully understand what your brand stands for and your core identity.

YOU ARE YOUR OWN BRAND

The Z. brand was built in just 15 months. Prior to selling million-dollar listings, I was selling homes in the southeast of Melbourne where my average house price was $400,000 to $600,000.

Before starting Z. Real Estate, people put a lot of fear in my head. I was told we wouldn't stand a chance of surviving in that market, but just because other people haven't done it, it doesn't mean that you can't do it. People's opinions don't have to be your reality. I believe a lot in innovation and change. We used social media for leverage and added every single client on all our social media platforms so they could follow our journey. We always over-delivered with every transaction. We wanted to build a brand to differentiate ourselves. We created the word *ZOLD* – instead of *sold*. In just a couple of months, it became the word of the town. The Z. Real Estate team ZOLD over

$500 million worth of real estate within our first year of operation, and we grew from a team of 5 to 12 in one year.

People now know our brand is different. We dress our business the same way we dress ourselves – sharp and expensive.

This is how we brand ourselves as wealth creation managers. We are your one-stop shop for all real estate needs: from finance, leasing, project marketing, commercial, house and land, conveyancing, building, architecture, and Zed Media. We don't just sell the home; we sell the lifestyle. We sell the dream. We sell the unattainable and make it easy for our clients.

"

PEOPLE'S OPINIONS DON'T HAVE TO BE YOUR REALITY.

"

DRESS TO IMPRESS

A person's physical appearance is paramount. Take care of your health and your well-being because how you present yourself is one of the most important aspects of self-promotion. Your physical appearance introduces you before you even say a word, as it shows how disciplined you are in life.

Think of yourself as an athlete suiting up for the big game, with your outfit based on the type of client you're meeting and the home you're showing. To do this, you have to read the room – something I revisit often in my professional and personal lives. Select an outfit based on the demographic of my client, even if that means overdressing on occasion. It's hard to go wrong with a nice suit and tie. When I hold open houses, I dress to match the design of the property. I want prospective buyers to feel like they're entering a specific lifestyle. For example, if I'm representing a beach house in Brighton with uninterrupted bay and city skyline views, I would choose a cream linen suit with a tropical shirt. If I'm showing a home in Toorak with impeccable interior design, I adjust my outfit to match the house's aesthetic. This way, when people arrive, I look the part of someone who would live there, helping them envisage themselves in the home and embracing the environment.

If you miscalculate the formality of your outfit, it's an immediate turn-off. As a salesperson, you need to be a chameleon in how you present yourself. Not only do you need to know your stuff, but you have to look the part to prove that you understand your clients' needs, wants, and overall ethos. You never want to leave anything to chance.

In addition to personal appearance, a flawless presentation of the home you're selling is vital. This includes how the home smells. I've entered homes where the seller claimed the home was ready but had left dirty laundry on the floor or dog waste in the garden. It's not always glamorous selling multimillion-dollar homes, but attention to detail can make all the difference.

PERSONAL BRANDING IS SUPER IMPORTANT, AND Z. REAL ESTATE KNOWS IT!

Having a strong personal brand can be the difference between your dreams falling apart and making them a reality. Planning to leave a traditional job after years can be daunting and scary! But we have the power to shape our own stories. We don't have to climb a boring ladder to fit someone else's idea of success. And to do that, you need to build your own personal brand.

This journey is unique to each of us. I've never regretted carving my own way, and I'm writing this book for those who want to navigate this new world and shine bright. Here's a crucial tip: If you don't build a brand that shows you're the go-to makeup artist, graphic designer, accountant, or personal chef, someone else will take that spotlight. The workplace is a huge opportunity waiting for you, but you need to put in the effort to grab it. Don't settle for second place. Don't let your competition overshadow you – it's your time to shine. Build your brand and see how far you can go!

"

WE HAVE THE POWER TO
SHAPE OUR OWN STORIES.

"

Take a moment to look around you. What do you see? Whether you're reading in a coffee shop, car, gym, plane, or at home on your couch, brands are all around us. It's fascinating to see how everything around us is a brand, subtly influencing how we see and experience things. Brands are all around us, whether they're objects, ideas, services, food, artists, designers, musicians, or athletes. We like to think we have full control over our choices, but we don't – not entirely, anyway. What we eat, wear, watch, follow, read, and listen to is all influenced by branding. Let's use this influence to elevate your business to new levels.

Before we dive into building your brand together, let's understand what a brand really is and review the steps we'll take to create yours.

I am very fortunate to sit down with wealthy clients all the time. They are entrepreneurs themselves, and I always ask them the question: What does branding mean to them? Here are some of the answers I gathered and learned from them. I would like to share them with you.

This is what I learned from John Moller, the founder of Repco: 'A brand is what people think about your company. It's like a shout and an echo. The shout is what you do, and the echo is what people think about what you do. That echo is your brand'.

FROM VISION TO VICTORY

When Maseeh and I started Z. Real Estate, our brothers, Qaiss and Tee, couldn't join us initially as they had their own finance company. Maseeh and I wanted a brand so powerful that it brought in business while we were sleeping.

What followed was an exciting period of reflection. We wanted to dig deep and examine our values, what we stood for, and what our purpose was. While every brand has a visual identity (and that's important), we didn't want to jump into names, colours, logos, and fonts until we uncovered the essence of the company we were building.

We thought about the image we wanted to project to the world and developed a clear vision of how to use media and property videos to create an entirely new way of Zelling. We reflected on who we were at our core and what unique qualities about our company should be showcased. The question was, how do we wrap all those ideas into a package that consistently makes it clear that Z. Real Estate is the go-to agency for buying and Zelling luxury properties all over Melbourne?

In addition to all that contemplation, we spent countless hours with our team designing a system to establish, grow, and maintain the foundation of our company – our brand, Z. Eventually, we came up with our very own Brand Strategy System, and it's become our in-house bible of branding. Our three-part system accomplishes a few key things: how to find and establish a core identity, how to create and use consistent content to generate brand awareness, and how to strategically develop a plan for sharing wins by 'shouting it from the mountaintop'.

This is the exact system we used to develop Z. Real Estate for all real estate needs, creating a one-stop shop and providing convenience for our clients through finance, construction, buyer advocacy, commercial, leasing, and the list goes on. Today, we are proud to say that we are the most followed real estate brand in the country.

Everyone doubted us and said we wouldn't last long in the luxury space. They believed we had no chance of survival, as there were agencies with long-term, strong relationships with every homeowner in Brighton. But Zelling anything to anyone starts with believing in yourself first before others buy into you.

It was only a matter of months before we became the talk of the town. Our ZOLD signs were up on boards all around Melbourne. We were getting calls from people saying, 'Hi, I think there's a spelling mistake on your boards'. Every time we knew, deep down, that our strategy was working.

After putting every penny I had into the business and finally building momentum, we decided to buy a building for $3 million and spend another $1 million on renovations. We faced many hurdles with the new purchase, and not long after, we were hit with COVID – just like the rest of the world. Of course, Melbourne broke a record for the highest number of lockdown days.

I realised that we can never predict what the universe has in store for us. We have to be ready to accept whatever it is – slow housing markets, inflation, ice storms, killer bees, vampires, supply chain issues, recessions, etc. – and move forward as best we can.

This is why crafting a personal brand is so important when it comes to protecting your livelihood. A brand isn't just a building, a store, a website, or a person – it's something much bigger. When you build a brand, you're making a vow to uphold the values at the core of that brand. You're making a promise to your customers that you'll always create the best possible experience for them. Those values and promises are something that can never be taken from you, not even during a hundred-year flood.

To borrow a thought from Dr George Berkeley, the philosopher and Anglican bishop from the 1600s: 'If a tree falls in the forest and no one is around to hear it, does it make a sound?' If someone is the best graphic designer, dog walker, yoga instructor, real estate agent, professional organiser, or personal chef and no one knows about it, does it matter?

The *Z.Talk* book and podcasts I release will help you build your brand from the ground up, and now I've made it my mission in life to help YOU unleash the brand that lives inside of you.

REDEFINING SUCCESS IN THE NEW ERA

Your brand is the heart and soul of your company. It is also the bright light that will guide you through the entirely new and unprecedented work environment we've all landed in. Every single thing we've been taught about success (and how to get it) has changed.

For a long time, we were told there was only ONE road that led to happiness, accomplishment, and money (and this road was available only to a specific group of privileged people – not women, not people of colour, and not people from other marginalised communities). All you had to do was ease down this magical yellow brick road and at the end you'd find a nice house, a new car, health insurance, holidays, and maybe even a luxury club membership all waiting under a rainbow with your name on it.

That road was restraining and confining. There wasn't room for everyone, and you were expected to keep your head down as you kept moving forward. If along the way you wanted to try something else – maybe follow your passion for writing or cooking or building interesting furniture – well then, step aside and enjoy your 'artistic' lifestyle, but don't expect to reap the same rewards.

Here's the good news: That old road to success is permanently closed. It has been ripped up and repaved by a new generation of workers who see things differently. Forget the straight lines. The new road has twists and turns, roundabouts, alleyways, and side streets, and you get to decide which direction you want to go in.

It gets better. That rusty old corporate ladder has been thrown in the bin because we don't need it. We can climb high all on our own.

Fast forward to today, and there's no room for basic; thinking big is essential to your survival.

Z. REAL ESTATE VALUES: BUILDING A BRAND THAT RESONATES

Your brand is everything. It's crucial to the success of your business. In this chapter, I've talked about uncovering your brand identity, personal branding, and how they each equate to positive promotion. Now let's discuss the alignment of your values with your brand and getting that to resonate with your clients and potential customers. Once you've got that equilibrium, your business will skyrocket to the next level.

- **Amplify together:** We support each other at our low points, and we never let our high points go to our heads. If one of us is behind, we are all behind. And when one of us succeeds, we ALL do.
- **Create for tomorrow:** We are future-obsessed and always look forward, creating to bring the future to today.
- **Be relentless:** We are not only tireless in the pursuit of achieving our goals, we are tenacious seekers of knowledge, never sacrificing personal growth for professional growth.
- **Disrupt for good:** We are the best at what we do because we never lose sight of the people and communities around us. Our voice carries above the rest, and we disrupt to have a positive, lasting impact.

As you begin this process, never forget that customers pay for values. Values matter more to consumers now than they ever have before. Consumers care about values such as carbon footprints, ethical sourcing, and social impact. Billions of dollars can be lost and a brand can be permanently damaged due to what some consumers view as a lapse in values.

Articulating your brand's values is about articulating the experience you want all your clients and customers to have.

Imagine you are a customer seeking out the exact service or product you offer. Picture the client or customer as they experience every aspect of your brand – logging onto your website, taking a meeting with you in a coffee shop, or walking into your physical office for the first time. Write down the ideal experience you want your customers to have and contemplate the following:

- **What do they see?** A well-designed website that is attractive, informative, and easy to navigate? A bridal shop that is light and airy? A café that's buzzing with activity, people working on laptops or having animated conversations, plates of delicious food everywhere? A smiling face that greets them at the local Starbucks where you're meeting to discuss dog-walking services?
- **What do they feel?** Pulling the right emotions out of your clients is an essential part of your brand experience. Is a bride's anxiety about planning her wedding being soothed? Does the café environment make a customer feel welcome and at home? Does the pleasant conversation and the positivity of the dog walker make the proud Labradoodle owner think, 'Oh, Muffin will be in great hands with this dog walker?'

- **How will you make the full experience a reality?** Now that you've imagined what it's like for a customer, ask yourself what key values need to be in place to make that experience a reality. For example, I knew if I wanted to be the go-to brand for luxury properties, I'd always have to be looking forward – using media in the most innovative way to sell properties. I knew that Z. Real Estate needed to be 'future-focused', so 'create for tomorrow' is one of our core values. Our clients know that Z. will always use the most innovative, creative, and groundbreaking methods to get properties sold for millions of dollars.

"

VALUES MATTER MORE TO CONSUMERS NOW THAN THEY EVER HAVE BEFORE.

"

THE EFFECT OF COLOUR ON BRANDING

Colour psychology is important, and colour is a useful tool to connect your brand with your audience. Colours can make us feel different emotions – both good and bad – and they play a big part in how customers see your brand and influence your choices. Understanding what each colour means can help you pick one that attracts your target audience.

While you can't predict how everyone will react to your colour choices you can use colour psychology to make better choices for your brand. Below is the same colour chart I used when choosing white and simple colours for all our marketing materials and sale signs. Simple, classy, and neutral colours are usually liked, with a bit of colour added here and there.

Each colour in the chart below has many shades that can express different feelings and ideas. Once you pick a colour family that matches your brand's personality, you can refine it until you find the right shade for you.

Colour Chart:
Red: Excitement, strength, love, energy
Orange: Confidence, success, bravery, friendliness
Yellow: Creativity, happiness, warmth, cheer
Green: Nature, healing, freshness, quality
Blue: Trust, peace, loyalty, competence
Pink: Compassion, sincerity, elegance, sweetness
Purple: Royalty, luxury, spirituality, ambition
Brown: Dependability, sturdiness, trustworthiness, simplicity
Black: Formality, drama, elegance, security
White: Cleanliness, innovation, simplicity, innocence, honesty

Tip: Don't overthink your logo colours.

While it's important to learn about colours that work well, you could spend forever looking for inspiration. Don't get lost in this process, or you may never finish. I recommend setting a reasonable deadline to keep things moving – one week at most if you're doing this on your own.

MARKETING

MARKETING FOR SUCCESS

Marketing is a crucial driver of sales, and both aspects must work hand-in-hand to take your business to the next level. In real estate, the success of your business doesn't only rely on how skilled you are at listing and selling properties, but also on how effectively you market yourself, your properties, and your services. In this chapter, I'll share marketing strategies which have helped my team grow both individually and professionally.

Easy and Effective Steps on Real Estate Marketing

The real estate industry has gone through many changes over the past decade. With growing competition among agents, it's important to have a solid understanding of both online and offline marketing to distinguish yourself from the crowd.

Set Yourself up for Social

In Australia, the following are the most active social media statistics, as at November 2025[1]:

- **Facebook** – 19,000,000 Monthly Active Australian Users
- **YouTube** – 18,500,000 Unique Australian Visitors per month
- **WhatsApp** – 13,000,000 Active Australian Users
- **Instagram** – 12,000,000 Monthly Active Australian Users
- **LinkedIn** – 6,500,000 Monthly Active Australian Users
- **Snapchat** – 6,400,000 Monthly Active Australian Users

Make sure you're present on all major platforms such as Facebook, Instagram, LinkedIn, YouTube, and even Snapchat (if you enjoy sharing property images). Engage with users, share positive press, and promote your properties regularly.

> PEOPLE ARE DRAWN TO AUTHENTIC, INSPIRATIONAL STORIES, SO DON'T BE AFRAID TO SHARE YOURS.

Keep an Eye on the Competition

Take note of what your competitors are doing in your area. Look at their websites, their social media activity, and how they market their properties. By avoiding their mistakes and learning from their successes, you'll be able to position yourself ahead of the competition.

Make Yourself Easy to Contact

Ensure that your contact information is clearly displayed on every page of your website. A well-designed 'Contact Us' page will make it easy for prospects to reach out to you.

Create a Killer Business Card

Your business card is a powerful marketing tool. Make sure it stands out and always have it on hand. You never know when an opportunity might present itself. I have two different types of cards. One is used for prospecting or door knocking and the other is a metal card which I hand out at networking events.

Make Use of Local Images

When marketing a property, don't just focus on the house. Get a drone photographer to showcase the neighbourhood as well. Highlight local amenities, parks, schools, shops and any other features that make the area desirable.

Create an Irresistible Content Offer to Capture Leads

Offer potential clients something of value in exchange for their contact details. Consider creating an eBook or guide on topics like 'Things to Consider Before Buying Your First Home' or 'The Most Valuable Features in a Home' or a Sellers' Guide that helps clients understand how to prepare a home for sale and what they should expect.

Hire a Professional Photographer

Investing in professional photography is essential for successful marketing. High-quality property photos significantly increase interest. Using a professional photographer makes all the difference; if you have poor quality photos of the home, people will miss its value and you will not receive many enquiries.

Local Sponsorship

Supporting local events, teams, or festivals can be a great way to market your services while giving back to your community. You'll not only build brand recognition but also establish a positive reputation as a community supporter.

Consider Going Niche

If you face heavy competition, try focusing on a niche market. Become the go-to real estate agent for specific groups, like families, boat shows, sports car club, pet owners, or retirees. Specialising can help you stand out and build a strong, loyal client base.

Use Emotional Storytelling

People connect with stories, so use emotional storytelling to highlight the benefits of a property. Show how it fits into the buyer's lifestyle and evoke positive emotions through compelling narratives and images.

Social Media Ads

Paid social media ads, particularly on Facebook and Instagram, can be an effective way to reach potential clients. With advanced targeting features, you can ensure your ads reach the right audience and generate more leads.

Advertise Your Properties in Local Papers

While digital marketing is important, don't underestimate the power of local newspapers and magazines. Write informative pieces, offer expert opinions, and make sure your name gets out there in the local community.

Get Branding

Branded merchandise like pens, drink bottles, and keychains can be a great way to spread your name. Giving these away at local events helps reinforce your brand.

Partner with Local Businesses

Building relationships with local businesses can create mutually beneficial partnerships. Consider offering co-branded marketing materials or hosting joint events to boost exposure for both parties.

Ask for Testimonials from Former Clients

A positive testimonial from a happy client can be one of the most effective ways to build trust with potential clients. Don't be shy about asking satisfied clients for a testimonial or even a photo to accompany it.

Create an Awesome Website

Your website should be your business's online home base. Ensure it is user-friendly, provides easy access to property details, and includes features like virtual tours, local area information, and contact details. Keep it updated and ensure it's optimised for both desktop and mobile use.

Give a Local Care Package After Closing

Show appreciation for your clients by sending them a local care package after closing. Include gift cards for local restaurants or tickets to local attractions. It's a thoughtful gesture that will help them remember you.

Keep in Touch

Don't just disappear after the sale. Stay in contact with past clients through occasional phone calls, anniversary cards, and holiday greetings. Keeping in touch shows that you care, and they are likely to make contact when they (or their friends) are looking to buy or sell again.

Interact with a Crowd

When speaking to a group, share your personal story. Make it engaging and relatable, and showcase how far you've come. People are drawn to authentic, inspirational stories, so don't be afraid to share yours.

Create a Referral System

Word-of-mouth is powerful in real estate. Set up a referral system and offer incentives to past clients who refer new business to you. Rewarding your loyal clients for spreading the word can lead to more opportunities.

SOCIAL MEDIA TIPS

Social media is part of our lives and it's here to stay. With this in mind, it would be foolish for anyone to overlook its impact on businesses. It's incredibly useful for reaching new clients, for engaging the community, and for building your business.

Make a Commitment to Social Media

Treat social media as a priority for your business. Set goals, create strategies, and monitor your progress. Whether your focus is brand awareness, sales, or somewhere in between, a clear plan will help you achieve your targets.

Establish Some Goals for Your Social Media Programme

Set specific, measurable goals for your social media efforts. Whether it's increasing engagement, growing followers, or generating leads, defining your objectives will help you evaluate the success of your social media campaigns.

Share Who You Are as a Brand or Business

People connect with authentic content. Share what makes you unique as an entrepreneur or business. Being transparent and human on social media will build stronger connections with your audience.

Make Time for Social Media

Consistency is key. Even small time investments on a regular basis can yield big results. Dedicate time to content creation and engagement each week to build a loyal community and grow your brand presence.

Engage with Your Customers

Listen to your followers and engage with them. Social media is an interactive platform, and building a conversation with your audience will help you understand their needs and build lasting relationships.

Hire Professional Photographers and Videographers

High-quality content is key to standing out. Invest in professional visuals, or if budget is a concern, improve your skills and equipment to create more engaging content yourself.

Passion = Great Content

The more passionate you are about a subject, the easier it will be to create engaging content. Find a topic that excites you and share your enthusiasm with your audience.

Learn from the Best

Follow industry leaders and competitors. Analyse their content and engagement strategies to find out what works, then adapt those ideas to fit your brand.

Engagement Drives Growth

Engaging with your audience fosters growth. Respond to comments, ask questions, and encourage others to share your content. Engagement is the key to building a strong, loyal community.

Don't Try to Be Everything

Focus on a clear niche for your social media efforts. Trying to cater to everyone will spread you too thin. Instead, focus on what you're passionate about, and your audience will connect with you on a deeper level.

"

FOCUS ON WHAT YOU'RE PASSIONATE ABOUT,
AND YOUR AUDIENCE WILL CONNECT
WITH YOU ON A DEEPER LEVEL.

"

SOCIAL MEDIA: THE LONG GAME

Social media offers one of the highest lead-to-close conversion rates, especially when compared to outbound marketing methods. The average social media user in Australia manages 5.54 accounts[2], and a significant portion of business comes through digital marketing.

Optimise Your Instagram Profile

Utilise Instagram Stories, which have seen a major uptick in business activity. Use bright colours, engage with your audience, and take advantage of Instagram's features for maximum impact.

Learn to Use Snapchat

Snapchat's vertical video format has higher completion rates, so embrace it. Use it regularly to get more comfortable with your content creation and engage with your audience.

Facebook Facts

With 3.07 billion[3] users worldwide, Facebook remains a critical platform. Use it for visual content, which gets 40 times more shares, and engage actively with your audience. Social media's power lies in consistency and interaction.

By mastering these strategies, you can create a strong online presence and build meaningful relationships with your audience, leading to greater success in your real estate business.

Making Videos That People Want to Watch

To get people to watch your videos, they don't need to be perfect or highly produced. They just need two important qualities: they should be clean and uncomplicated.

Keep it simple and clear! Just follow these three easy guidelines:

1. Make sure the speaker can be heard.
2. Show the speaker's face.
3. Include key visuals.

This is very important. You don't need high production values to succeed. A video can be simple and still connect with people. Just stick to these *BASIC* rules and don't get distracted by fancy details. (If you want to make a big film, go for it! But if you want to grab attention for your brand and make more money, this is all you need.)

Always remember to keep it straightforward and clear. For example, the time to launch videos keeps getting shorter. On YouTube, you now have just 59 seconds to tell your story or share your message. This means there's no room for fluff; you need a clear and simple message.

Let's talk about the message you want to share. You have only a few seconds to grab your audience's attention, and the next five seconds will decide if they keep watching. That's less time than it takes to cough! To tackle this short time frame, use this formula:

1. **Start with a Catchy Intro:** Begin with a clear statement that shows what the viewer will learn. Using a number indicates there are several tips. For example: 'Four tips from a successful leader.'

2. **Share a Personal Story:** Facts are important, but stories create a real connection. Think of your story as a way to lead to your main points. For example: 'I once flew with a millionaire who was closing a big deal. After the call, he said to me... *add in your wise quote here.*'
3. **Motivate Your Audience:** After sharing your ideas, end with a clear call to action that inspires your listeners. Show them how your message can help. For example: 'To succeed, use this important advice in your life starting today!'

Finally, remember that social media is about trying things out. The sooner you get comfortable with this, the better. While you can track a video's success, no one can predict what content will become popular. Pay attention to what works for you, but stay open to experimenting. By focusing on being clean and keeping it simple, you can try new things.

TELL STORIES WITH MEANING

It's important to understand what your audience wants and needs to build a strong brand. To make your storytelling effective, try to see things from their perspective. Who are you trying to reach? Imagine that person in front of you and ask yourself, what would make them click on our video? What kind of tone would they like? What are they looking for on social media?

How can we make our story more entertaining to keep them watching... or even better, get them to call their mum and suggest that if they're thinking about selling their house in Brighton, they should contact Z. Real Estate? That's the goal. Build and keep that connection by being consistent, and in the end, you'll create more business for yourself.

While pretty pictures can catch our eye, social media often shows a fake version of life, only sharing the best moments. Being real online means accepting that you don't have to be perfect all the time. It's great to share your successes, but people also want to see the real you.

Many influencers have found that sharing everyday banalities can connect better with their audience. For example, a simple video of someone walking with a baby can get more views than fancy posts. This shows that people appreciate honesty more than perfection.

While stunning photos are still nice to see, sharing your daily life – like being a parent or facing challenges – makes you more relatable. Embracing your flaws and showing reality can help you connect with others. So, forget about being perfect and celebrate the beautiful mess of life!

MAXIMISING CONNECTIONS: THE CRUCIAL ROLE OF SOCIAL MEDIA IN REAL ESTATE AND SALES

The first trick to start attracting followers is being active in your postings. Your posts need to be integrated with who you are on a daily basis. It doesn't matter whether you're an account manager, a yoga teacher, or a salesperson; always give something to your followers – a laugh, a piece of good information, or an intimate peek at your life. Use the same account name on all platforms, and also keep the content the same or very similar on all by reposting from one to another. It's really the only way to be able to manage it all while simultaneously expanding.

"

YOUR POSTS NEED TO BE INTEGRATED WITH WHO YOU ARE ON A DAILY BASIS.

"

The Secret of Sharing: It's not just one way; it goes both ways. Someone is following you, and in return, you need to give them something. If you give them more than your competition, your followers will grow. So, for every instance you brag about business or a new record, make it inspirational and include a good photo. For the next five posts, only offer interesting things that aren't bragging.

Whatever we put out there is a demonstration of how we see ourselves, a self-portrait of our lives. My social media – @zednasheet – is the official record of where I've been and where I'm going. You can tell a lot about a person online. What someone posts says so much about who they are, but also about how they want to be perceived (which is usually two different things).

One might call your social media profile a modern and more colourful autobiography, with juicy contributors offering their likes and comments – most positive and some negative. We must always be authentic – people can smell a fake.

Several of my top competitors have bought followers. It's getting more common, and I find it tacky. Although I don't support it, I understand why they are doing it. In a competitive industry, which is so numbers-driven, they want to win the game.

How can you tell if someone is faking it and buying followers or likes? Their numbers jump magically in an hour or overnight.

The one thing no one can buy, at least so far, is a comment. By looking at the number of comments, you can see who is fake or not. I've come up with a formula for the average Instagram post: two to five percent of your followers like your post and 30 percent of likers will comment. Therefore, the problem for the faker who has 500 real followers and buys 50,000 followers is that he only gets 16 likes yet still only has three comments on the post. And there is no way he can increase that.

Here are some of the trends I see in social media right now:

- Social media investment is becoming a necessity, not a luxury. Traditional forms of selling, marketing, and prospecting are becoming secondary to social media tactics. The results speak for themselves.
- A continuum of social engagement is vital. The first step to success in the crazy social world is to get by the one-and-done hump. You need to change the paradigm of thinking from single-shot activity to a continuum of ongoing engagements.
- You need to be everywhere your customer or influencer is. Don't think about a single network. Your prospect is social everywhere on the web, and your social activity must behave in the same way. The experience should be consistent, and the data synchronised across all web platforms.

- Multimedia and visual storytelling are key. Start thinking like a storyteller! Turn your life or agenda into a personal story with heroes and villains from your personal or professional position. Smart content is powerful and grabs eyeballs.
- Content must be mobile-friendly. It's important to go the extra mile when thinking about the content and how people experience it. It should come as no surprise that mobile is king when it comes to social media. Be thoughtful and strategic as you engage and participate on social media with the mobile user in mind.
- Response/engagement is crucial. Get to know your audience and understand both their business and personal interests. Offer content that entertains as well as helps them meet the challenges of life. We live in the era of instant everything! Success belongs to the quick and the nimble.

LEVERAGING YOUTUBE FOR REAL ESTATE SUCCESS: BUILDING YOUR BRAND WITH VIDEO CONTENT

When most people think of social media, they probably think of Instagram and Facebook. Before we discuss those, I should also mention that YouTube can serve as an outstanding learning tool, and creating video content can increase your profile and audience to bring attention to what you have to offer or sell. People are building entire careers by posting YouTube videos. There are more than four billion daily views on YouTube. That's the equivalent of more than half the world's population watching a video every day. If you're a plumber and create a video on 'How to Fix a Leaky Toilet', you're not just helping someone solve their problem; you are also setting yourself up as an expert and, for the people near you, as the one to call when there's a burst pipe. If you're a real estate agent who provides video tours of your properties, you're not just showcasing your properties; you're highlighting yourself as a professional in the marketplace.

According to a recent survey by Marketing LTB[4] 68 percent of customers viewing a video online will make a purchasing decision based on that clip. So, make yourself the expert in your field by creating engaging content that appeals to our visual nature. Share information about your product or service that establishes a following. If it's clever, you might even go viral, and that will bring you a bottomless pool of clients and buyers.

MASTERING INSTAGRAM: YOUR KEY TO SUCCESS IN SOCIAL MEDIA MARKETING

Yep, Instagram is the go-to place for marketing now. This cute sibling of Facebook was created mainly for sharing mobile photos and later videos with friends. It's simple: snap a pic, spruce it up with easy digital filters, and add a caption. Then the pic appears in the feed for your followers, with no ads (yet!), no clutter, and no distractions.

Here are six things I adore about Instagram:

1. Unlike Facebook, the posts are perfectly arranged in order. I follow 231 people, and each time I check Instagram, I see their posts in the order they were posted. It's based on time,

not anything else. So, if you scroll back enough, you can see every pic from everyone you follow. It's fresh and cool. Instagram users are active and attentive. There are fewer inactive users, and the active ones use it a lot. It's super engaging and fun, and users open the app more times a day than any other social network. The vibe is trendier, more stylish, and gets more notice.

2. A picture is a powerful selling tool. Instagram shows one image at a time. One square of colour. A well-captured Instagram photo speaks more than a thousand words or 140,000 characters. My Instagram feed includes awesome contrasts, from top outdoor photographers to personal feeds of other celebrities, and everything in between.
3. The app is brilliant in its simplicity. The Instagram scroll was made akin to slot machines, making it fun to tap through the pics with your fingers on the screen.
4. Its user-friendly filters can add an artistic touch to each photo, making it seem like a shot by a professional photographer without the heavy gear.
5. The likes are motivating. Instagram thrives on likes, creating a sort of competition with yourself (or with your peers). In my early Instagram days, hitting 100 likes on a photo thrilled me. Now, not reaching 10,000 likes on a favourite picture disappoints me. It's all relative.
6. It's easy to be spontaneous and see spontaneity in others on Instagram. If used wisely, Instagram opens a window to your true self, revealing your artistic side, your heart,

and how you view the world. Beauty lies in the eye of the beholder, and two individuals may capture one object differently in a photo. It's a genuine snapshot of where you are, without worrying about who might see it, and that's freeing and, at the same time, connecting. I feel a genuine connection with people on Instagram, even those I've never met and may never meet, because by following them, I observe their journeys, dreams, travels, and intimate moments. And I don't merely 'like' it; I love it.

POP QUIZ!

1. Do we acknowledge that social media is here to stay? Yes or No.
2. Do we think it's going to become more and more of who we are? Yes or No.

If you answered yes to any of the above, you need to kickstart or boost your social media presence now. Use social media as a potent sales tool to pave your way to success in whatever you're pursuing.

Now that we know the basics of popular platforms, let's delve into some universal tips to grab attention, gain more followers and likes:

1. **Always include a photo**. A photo speaks volumes and catches attention instantly. Always, always include a photo! Even if it's not on Instagram, add a photo. A text-only post is dull and doesn't engage as well, resulting in fewer likes. The clearer and more captivating, the better. Know what draws eyes. Animals, babies, nature, sunsets, sunrises, skyscrapers, ocean waves, and sometimes semi-nude photos grab attention. Everyone loves an adorable dog. Share that. People love pets. Follow the five-hour rule. Limit your posts to two within five hours. Posting more than that can turn people off. Plus, repeating the same theme multiple times is a big no. For instance, if you announce an engagement with a 'He asked me' post that gets a lot of likes, avoid quickly posting 'I'm in shock' and then a beaming 'I'm so happy' pic. Once you get a like, you don't need to say it again and again about the same thing in a day.
2. **Make your followers feel involved**. Yes, social media can revolve around showing off, promoting, and selling, but there are subtle ways to do it right. A major no-no is posting a pic of a group and saying, 'Great night with friends'. This might alienate your followers. They'd feel left out, excluded from the party. They weren't at the table. They sat in their dark rooms staring at the screen while you showed off your fabulous life.
3. **Don't flaunt stuff in people's faces**. If you want to engage your followers, make them a collaborator. It's more humble,

adds depth, and invites a connection. This is crucial because, as we agreed earlier, there's no point in posting if no one sees it and it doesn't go up in the feed.

4. **Experiment with variety**. Repetition kills on social media. People remember well, and if you keep repeating, they lose interest. I consciously alternate between five themes:
   » Sales-related content – a record, a new listing, hitting $30 million in sales, book promotions, etc.
   » A beautiful Melbourne CBD photo or from my travels, paired with a Z.Talk description.
   » Images of my dog, Mr. ZOLD. I cried for three days when he passed away, and I'm usually not an emotional person.
   » Occasional selfies, sometimes casual, outside, like on a run or a hike, avoiding mirror selfies.
   » If you're in a location like a small island, don't post too much of the same scene. Only the first post will gather many likes. Don't flood with ten pics of the same beach before saying goodbye.
   » Each post of similar content, like lunch, beach swim, umbrella selfie, cabana massage, or a sunset dinner leads to gradual disinterest, unless you take extraordinarily captivating pics. Less is more, always.
5. **Be bold**. Social media is about visibility. You want as many eyes on your content as possible. You want people talking. That doesn't mean you have to post a video of you and your boss twerking at the office party, but if you do, do it with flair and own it – your post could become the talk of the town. Every now and then, step out of your comfort zone

a bit. It grabs attention, and though the post might not get as many likes as expected, it will set you apart. Remember when Miley Cyrus twerked and everyone thought it was her downfall? There was a storm of criticism, but she gained two million followers overnight. She's now the world's top-selling artist.

6. **Engage with others**. I like posts, yes, with the thumbs-up button. I like every single comment people make, even if there are thousands on a post. It may take time, but the like is my acknowledgment that I've seen their comment. And when possible, I try to respond to comments. Social media can sometimes feel like everyone's talking without listening. Step into the crowd, engage with your followers. Few realise it should be a dialogue. Everyone wants to be heard, validated, and connected.
7. **Don't fall into the trap of waiting for buyers to show up and buy**. Why are you on social media? If it's not for updating your folks on your life, call them instead. If you aim to sell, learn to play the game on social media with style. Start building your following before your rivals. As social media progresses, the link between your follower interaction and your results will become more apparent. How well you engage your followers will directly impact your outcomes. To me, social media is where I pitch all my Z.Talk.
8. **But, most importantly, those posts (my social media endeavours) act as markers ahead of me and tracks of my journey behind**. They serve dual purposes in my life, one

visible and one deep within my spirit, swinging back and forth between the two.

9. **Social media nudges me towards the future.** Oddly, social media guides my decisions towards a happier life. I know some folks may dislike shaping their choices based on faceless opinions, but your followers like what you like. Social media steers us towards the meaningful, significant aspects of life, promoting connection and engagement.
10. **Social media helps me reflect on the past.** Life is a series of fleeting moments. Every tick, every second, swiftly flies past us, and these pics, captions, comments, and likes form a private diary. It's yours, irreplaceable. You can't turn back time, but you have snippets to look back on. **If nothing else, view your social media as a vibrant diary that can also bring in cash.** Now, go post something and tag me in it.

"

SOCIAL MEDIA IS ABOUT VISIBILITY. YOU WANT AS MANY EYES ON YOUR CONTENT AS POSSIBLE.

"

MASTERING FACEBOOK FOR BUSINESS GROWTH

I look at Facebook like a big high school reunion where you see old friends and a few relatives, and everyone is telling one another how great his or her life is. If I'm a little smart, I look at it as a genius sales tool. At times, Facebook might make you feel inadequate, like your life isn't adding up to the hype of other people's lives. But get over any feelings of inadequacy and get yourself in the game. You have to be on Facebook, and you have to grow an audience there.

Let's look at the latest stats[5]:

- Facebook has 3.07 billion users.
- Users spend almost 20 hours a month on Facebook.

Facebook uses a complicated algorithm that they have rewritten a 1000 times to choose its 'Top Stories' amid anyone's feed. Basically, the algorithm controls what you are and are not seeing. No one really knows the exact formula of how you get listed the highest – Facebook keeps it guarded but I've done some surveys and learned a few things. Every seven minutes, Facebook measures how many likes one of your posts has received. It also measures how many comments you have, as well as who is commenting and who is liking. At seven minutes, your post will come pretty high up in basically everyone's feed, and then it starts either dying or growing. There are many theories regarding what time of day (or night) one should post to get the best traction on Facebook. I've found the ideal time is around 8:00 am in Melbourne because everyone checks their phones or socials before work or around 5:00 pm. It's a weird game of roulette, though, and that is why Facebook can get so addictive: You never know why some posts become successful and some don't. You think you know, and then you realise you really don't. Just like a slot machine, it's rather unpredictable, but I will share with you my secrets to make it less so.

Facebook's algorithm is complicated because they want to make money. And that's done by boosting or promoting a page to force acceleration in the algorithm. This is fairly inexpensive and fun because it takes out some of the unpredictability.

The Difference Between A Profile And A Page And Engagement

Before we go into advertising on Facebook, let me explain the difference between a profile and a page. A profile is where it all started: your personal portal with your name. Your profile is great to keep connected with your friends and family, but since you realise that you are your business, you should definitely have a page. The page gives you a wider range of options; it makes it easier to grow a larger audience and advertise, and most importantly, it lets you focus on business promotion while keeping connected with it all. Facebook will give you the numbers. With a simple click of a button, you can view your page's 'Insights' – statistics on your most successful post, your number of likes, the reach of your content, number of new followers, clicks, and shares, really all the data about your page. There are nice graphs to see these numbers over time. Basically, you get to see what's working and what's not. In sales, that is a valuable tool.

Historically (10 years is a long time in social media's evolution), it was complicated to advertise on Facebook, but since becoming a publicly traded company, they've been forced to put programming and design muscle behind their platform so the common man can easily advertise there. I do it more and more because you can make it super precise and targeted and then follow up on its success with Insights. And you should, too. YouTube has some great video tutorials on how to advertise on Facebook. Take them. When you figure it out, it's a powerful promotional tool.

When you're marketing something, selling something, or even talking about your Afghan meatballs, you want as many people to see the post as possible. And the right people. Facebook makes this possible, and you can choose if you want to pay for views (impressions) or actions (clicks and/or likes). The more people you reach, the more people will share your posts on Facebook, which takes your reach one step further. Sharing, much like retweeting, is the act of somebody reposting what you've posted. Instantly, your post will show up – as you – in the feeds of people who aren't even following you. It is all silent, digital, and instant, but so, so important. Call it gossiping, bragging, educating, or what you will, but it feels nice to have something you posted talked about by a lot of people.

Facebook allows active engagement. To buy a full-page ad in a newspaper that is actually read by a million people and not thrown out or flipped through would cost a fortune, too. And don't even get me started on how long it would take to go knock on a million doors.

EMBRACE TECHNOLOGY: THE KEY TO MODERN SELF-PROMOTION

In today's digital world, embracing technology is essential for self-promotion. The bigger your digital network and social following, the greater your outreach – especially with younger generations. Currently, buyers in their 20s and early 30s are using social media platforms like Instagram and TikTok for communication and research. On the other hand, slightly older consumers tend to rely more on Facebook and LinkedIn. The younger generations are all about multitasking – they can do homework, watch TV, browse YouTube, laugh at TikTok videos, and chat with dozens of friends on Snapchat, all while acing their grades. It's unbelievable how much they can juggle at once. As a marketer, you need to be consistent with your content because sometimes it takes seeing something multiple times – five, ten, or even twenty times – for someone to take action.

Social media has undoubtedly generated significant leads for us, and we've made substantial sales through it – up to $9.7 million. While the bulk of our business still comes from our sphere of influence and established client base, closing additional sales through Facebook, Instagram, and TikTok can turn into a steady, investable income stream. For example, if you make ten sales totalling $250,000 one year, and 12 the next year, that's an additional $50,000 in revenue – a 20 percent increase. That extra income can be reinvested into your business, helping it grow.

In the fast-paced world we live in, staying innovative and evolving your approach to self-promotion is crucial. At Z. Real Estate, we have a dedicated digital marketing team. We're also creating artificial intelligence tools to help us better understand the people who engage with our content. By identifying those who are likely interested in purchasing real estate, we can connect with them more effectively and grow our business through modern technology.

"

IN TODAY'S DIGITAL WORLD, EMBRACING TECHNOLOGY IS ESSENTIAL FOR SELF-PROMOTION.

"

BUILD A NETWORK

If you don't target the right audience, marketing and advertising won't yield results. The key is to find your network and then figure out how to make your name matter. Your pay cheque is a direct reflection of your efforts.

In sales, everyone is a potential buyer, and you want to ensure that buyers can easily reach you. This means your email address and phone number must be clearly displayed on your website and social media. For me, one challenge of being a real estate agent on TV is that all of my contact information is public, which means I receive a lot of irrelevant calls. But, being in the service industry, I need to remain accessible to everyone.

Building a brand and a trusted reputation takes time, and it only takes one mistake to destroy it. That's why you have to treat your reputation like gold.

As your brand grows, it's important to pick one or two areas to focus on and become an expert. In real estate, some agents specialise in knowledge about specific architectural styles or renowned architects, like Christopher Doyle and Nicholas Day. Others become respected advisers by mastering specific areas, whether it's the market, building trends, or local neighbourhoods.

Another key to building your network is recognising that every person you meet could lead to an opportunity. It's essential to talk to people, listen with an open mind, and gather important details. It could be someone sitting next to you on a plane – it's happened to me more than once. Just recently, I got a call from a gentleman who had been my seatmate on a flight to the Gold Coast a month ago. He was calling to get my opinion on selling his mother's house. Not only did I give my advice, but I also referred him to Z. Money, our in-house finance team, and ended up listing the property.

I wouldn't have listed that property if I hadn't made that connection initially.

MASTERING YOUR SCRIPTS FOR SUCCESS

The most successful real estate agents likely have one thing in common: they practise their scripts. 'Scripts: New Ways to Handle Old Objections'[6] is an insight from several industry experts on how real estate professionals can better tackle their scripts, from practice to execution.

Strong communication is the key to making transactions work, and in real estate, strong communication boils down to strong conversational intelligence – especially when it comes to executing scripts.

ZED'S WAY TO MAKE THE MOST OF YOUR SCRIPTS

1. **Confident, but Never Lie.** I can't emphasise enough how important it is to be straightforward and give straight answers when a client asks you a question. Move forward with confidence, but never fake it. Clients will respect you more for your honesty. Then, when you follow up with the correct information, they will trust you more and appreciate your honesty.
2. **Listen First.** 'It's not about memorising, it's about listening'. Pay attention to your clients' words to understand the right script to use and build a stronger rapport. Is your client more focused on statistics? Use numbers and facts. Are they more emotionally connected to their future home? Appeal to that sentiment. Listen and respond accordingly. The script will only get you so far.
3. **Ask Questions.** Stop talking and start asking questions that are relevant to the client. Respond to their needs, be an adviser and guide them towards the right way once you have acknowledged what your client is after. Shift the conversation from simply presenting information to engaging the client in a way that makes them feel heard and valued.

4. **Know the 'Why'.** The most important part of the script process is determining buyer motivation. Understand the 'why' before you respond to the 'what'. Are your buyers just curious, or are they determined to buy a home tomorrow? Ask questions to understand how to move forward. Creating an emotional response in buyers builds a bond, making it more than just a transaction.
5. **Practise Makes Perfect.** Practise your scripts with colleagues or in front of a mirror before a meeting. I do role-playing with my team every Thursday from 10:00 am to 1:00 pm non-negotiable. No one should be too busy to practise. Schedule it and make it happen.
6. **Always Be On.** When someone is paying for your time, you need to deliver. Clients expect you to be on your A-game, enthusiastic, and engaged, no matter your mood. I always say my day is going 'unbelievably' well – clients assume you've just ZOLD or had a record-breaking day. You're always performing, and they deserve nothing less than your best.

"

MOVE FORWARD WITH CONFIDENCE,
BUT NEVER FAKE IT. CLIENTS WILL
RESPECT YOU MORE FOR YOUR HONESTY.

"

ZED'S TIPS FOR SUCCESS

Confidence isn't about walking into a room thinking you're better than everyone; it's walking in without having to compare yourself to anyone at all.

Here is a list of the **Top Six Qualities** that you, as a salesperson, should practise and perfect until they become an unconscious part of who you are:

1. **Be Completely and Totally Prepared.** Always study your client before the meeting. Learn their hobbies, know how many children they have, build rapport and they will respect you and take you seriously. Have a clear idea of how you are going to help them. Expect that they are going to have questions for you as well as objections. Be so prepared that you have an answer to each and every question they may have.
2. **Be Happy and Enthusiastic.** Put a big smile on your face and listen to something positive before a meeting. Let your prospect see that you are excited to meet them and you're looking forward to doing business with them.

3. **Bring Everything You Have to Offer.** Show your true value. Offer more than just getting a great price, make clients feel special. Be available 24/7 for the vendor and also for the buyers wishing to inspect after hours as well. If you're an agent who charges low commission then it can backfire on you. Nobody wants to deal with the cheapest; people think there must be something wrong. Why is it cheap? You will lose business like this. If you don't value you, how do you expect your client to value you?
4. **Always Listen to the Customer.** Listen to clients very closely as they are the ones paying your bills. And you want word-of-mouth business from them to be referred to their friends and families. Be an adviser not a pushy salesman. Listen, acknowledge, and respond according to what they are saying.
5. **Dress Professionally and Have Great Hygiene.** Always dress to impress, look sharp and present yourself professionally. When you present yourself well, your clients will enjoy working with you. Everyone will appreciate the effort you have put in to make yourself presentable and they judge you in the right way. You will not be forgotten.
6. **Never Start or Get Into an Argument with a Customer.** It takes a big person in life to say thank you and sorry. Never make the customer look bad, even if they're wrong or rude. If you feel like the customer is being insulting or rude, gently ask if there is something you've done to make them angry. Most times, they will tell you. Apologise sincerely and ask if they still want a meeting or would

like to reschedule. If they insist on being rude, make your apologies and leave. But *never* lose your cool. This is a small world, and it will get around – always act like a professional.

Here are two of my favourite quotes that have made a big impact in my life.

'The major key to your better future is you.'

Jim Rohn

'Take advantage of every opportunity to practice your communication skills so that when important occasions arise, you will have the gift, the style, the sharpness, the clarity, and the emotions to affect other people.'

Jim Rohn

“

CONFIDENCE ISN'T ABOUT WALKING INTO A ROOM THINKING YOU'RE BETTER THAN EVERYONE; IT'S WALKING IN WITHOUT HAVING TO COMPARE YOURSELF TO ANYONE AT ALL.

”

YOU, YOUR MINDSET AND SUCCESS

'You see things, and you say, "Why?"
But I dream of things that never were, and I say, "Why not?"'
George Bernard Shaw,
Irish playwright and critic

FIGURE OUT EXACTLY WHAT YOU WANT

According to the 2021 Australian Census Data, the population of Australia is 25.5 million[7], and one in six (15 percent) Australians are unhappy in their job, with a staggering 89 percent wanting to pursue a different career[8]. It's easy to say, 'If you're unhappy, just look for another job', but for some people, it's not that simple. It's dependent on someone's level of education, skills, and area of knowledge. Australia is a beautiful country, and most people are content with their life and jobs or are in their comfort zone. But when you don't follow your passion and focus only on the money, you will not enjoy your job. The question isn't about how much you're getting paid, but what you're becoming from that job while you're in it, and how it helps you develop the necessary skills to reach your end goal.

We are often content and happy with what we have as long as it pays the bills. However, we can't compare our technology or infrastructure to that of Dubai, the U.S., or even some European countries. We aren't particularly innovative and tend not to embrace change – that's why we watch American reality TV and movies. Honestly, I can't remember the last time I watched an Australian movie. We have it too good here, but in terms of lifestyle and raising a family, we are blessed and fortunate to have such amazing opportunities and beautiful places to visit. We often travel outside Australia, but most of us haven't even explored this country. In my eyes, it's the most beautiful country in the world.

But really, you should have no excuses not to make it. The only person standing in the way of achieving your goals is the bullshit stories you tell yourself. Too many people are content here. We've got shelter, food, Netflix, Facebook, Instagram, and TV to keep us distracted forever.

YOU NEVER KNOW WHAT YOU'RE CAPABLE OF

You never know what's possible. We all don't know what we're capable of until we push past our limits. Sometimes in life, you have to decide – at least one more time – to be *The Little Engine That Could*, even when you think you can't. When you decide to do something great, your life takes on new meaning. You instantly chart a new course. Your life goes from ordinary to extraordinary. You decide that what you do will make a difference, that what you do will matter, and that will give everything you do all that you've got. If you're going to go down, then you're not going down without a fight. But failure isn't even an option. It's not even on your radar. In your mind, you can see the prize – front and centre – and larger than life. It's the path, and you're on it. With all your might, and maybe even a little magic, you'll move whatever mountain stands in your way. It's onward and upward. It's time to do something great.

The truth is, nobody is perfect, and you can't be or have everything. You are you, and there is only one person who looks like you in this lifetime. That's your biggest point of difference in life and in your business. With that said, you can't satisfy every client you meet. Nobody is perfect. I bet you any money that even if Jesus came down to earth tomorrow, some people would still say, 'He needs a haircut'.

Money doesn't define who you are, and it doesn't buy happiness. It buys you experiences that put a smile on your face. Money just makes living comfortable, but it's not everything. Let's use the great Elvis Presley or Michael Jackson as examples. They had everything they could ask for and could buy anything, but who knows if they were happy in their personal life? I say, 'More money, more problems'.

So, you better be in a field that you're passionate about. If you follow your passion, you'll have more chances of succeeding. You'll make more sacrifices to get to your end goal. There's no point being in a field if you're not passionate about it, as Steve Jobs famously said, 'The only way to do great work is to love what you do.'

And then there's Richard Branson: 'There is no greater thing you can do with your life and your work than follow your passions in a way that serves the world and you.' Or, better yet: 'Choose a job you love, and you will never have to work a day in your life.'

My passion wakes me up every day, and thanks to my passion, I look forward to picking up the phone and closing that hard client that nobody else wanted to take on. If it weren't for my passion, I wouldn't wake up excited every morning to go to work. I look forward to my next deal, I look forward to getting rejected, I look forward to adding value and dealing with problems. I look forward to guiding people on creating wealth for them, and people can feel how passionate I am about my job and their properties.

Growing up, my brother and I were very passionate about cricket, so we joined the local team. My brother got selected to bowl and bat, and I was the benchwarmer, or the water boy. But I even enjoyed sitting on the bench and watching the game because I wanted to be around people who were passionate about the sport and be surrounded by that energy so I could grow and learn from it. By now, you've probably figured out that I must be a pretty good sportsman. I'm not really into sports, but anything I do, if I'm not passionate about it, I don't even try or waste my time on it. It's your passion that makes you stand out above the crowd. Passion will not help you if you don't have your goals written down. You need to make sure your goal is achievable, realistic, and that you have an exit plan.

I wasn't sure what I wanted to do when I finished high school. I didn't know anything about real estate, and I didn't even know what appraisals were. I had no knowledge of the industry, and why would someone hand over their biggest asset to the new kid on the block with no experience and knowledge about the industry? It was very challenging for me, and I would get nervous every time I dealt with a client. I failed for a good three years without even a dollar to my name. The only thing that helped me through this time was goals and clear direction of where I was going. I didn't want to give up. I told myself, 'If he or she can do it and make great money, I can do it too. Even better'. Goals give you a sense of direction, and they give you a purpose to live and work for.

"

IF YOU FOLLOW YOUR PASSION, YOU'LL HAVE MORE CHANCES OF SUCCEEDING.

"

I wasted time at jobs that weren't right for me, but they were all stepping stones. I worked as a hot dog boy outside nightclubs in Melbourne when I was only 14 years old, barely being able to speak English properly. I worked from 8:00 pm to 5:00 am. I worked in hospitality for ten hours before getting fired. The owner told me I wasn't made for hospitality. I worked at Telstra, selling mobile phones. I knew these jobs weren't right for me, but they were still valuable because they showed me what I didn't want.

After having these jobs and working for others, I knew I wasn't made for taking orders from other people or being in an environment where there were no guarantees. It didn't matter if you were an employee or not – you were just another number to them. I didn't want to be part of it. I knew I had more to give in life, and I started to think like an entrepreneur. I told myself, 'Our parents migrated to Australia to make something of ourselves, not to take orders from people who aren't even in control or nowhere near the mindset and vision I have'.

How can you work for someone who has no goals, no drive, no motivation, no hunger, no vision, and is happy to pay the bills and recently got promoted after 15 years in the organisation? That was definitely not how I wanted to pursue my dream and career. The first step is to write down your goals, pursue them, learn from your mistakes, and keep pursuing them until you reach your destination.

As an agent, you'll need to have an effective plan of attack – clearly defined goals that are not only achievable but that will also move the needle for your business. Goals are a great way to guarantee your success in the year ahead. I have my daily goals, weekly goals, monthly goals, yearly goals, and to the point where I've planned my next 21 years. One of my goals is to build the tallest real estate tower in the world, where it will be a one-stop shop for all your real estate needs – whether it's finance, architecture, building, town planning, engineering, tradies, car dealerships, barber shops – anything to do with real estate or land, I want it inside the Z. TOWER.

At the end of the day, goals are what gives you direction in life. By setting goals for yourself, you give yourself a target to shoot for. This sense of direction is what allows your mind to focus on a target, and, rather than wasting energy shooting aimlessly, it allows you to hit your target and reach your goal.

"

GOALS ARE WHAT GIVES YOU DIRECTION IN LIFE.

"

ZELLING IS A DECISION

Selling well is your decision. It doesn't matter if you don't have the skill set or the knowledge to deal with high-end clients, and it doesn't matter if the company you work for doesn't have proper training systems or support your vision. Every expert was once a beginner. Life is a journey, not a destination. It takes time to grow, but you are the one who must decide to self-educate and decide to be great.

When the property market is hot, anyone can sell. You don't even need an agent to represent you – properties would sell themselves if they're priced right. But in a tough market like today, this is when you know who a true negotiator is. Anyone can point to a kitchen and say, 'Here's the kitchen. Isn't it nice and big?'

Come on. How about, 'This kitchen offers ample space. The chef of the family will love it! You've got Gaggenau appliances, a double oven, a steamer, a coffee machine, double sinks, bronze tapware, marble benchtops with waterfall edges, soft-closing cabinets – so when you have a bad day at work, you can smash the drawers and nobody will hear it. Metallic glass splashback, a walk-in butler's pantry, tons of storage – it's custom-designed to suit anyone who loves entertaining. I love this kitchen. I wish I'd built something similar at my house.'

When you sell, sell with passion. Be authentic. Be excited. You need to educate them, and you need to believe it to achieve it.

I've attended many open homes where the agent registers your name and lets you walk through the home by yourself. How are you supposed to know as a buyer about the fixtures and fittings used in the home? As an agent, it's your responsibility to hold their hand, walk them through the home, and paint a picture of what it's like living there. Most buyers may not see the vision on their own. Give them some interior advice, build rapport, and qualify the clients so you're not wasting your time.

BUILDING A LIFE THAT MATTERS: PURPOSE, INTEGRITY AND THE COURAGE TO BECOME YOUR BEST SELF

Let's get real: You're not here just to exist. You're here to become the truest, highest expression of yourself.

You don't need to have every detail of your life figured out. But you *do* need a direction. A vision. Because if you're not in the driver's seat, life will gladly take the wheel – and drive you somewhere you never wanted to go.

Don't just coast through life. Don't just 'see what happens'. Set your GPS. Know your destination. Own your journey.

Not everyone will be famous. But everyone has the potential to be great – because greatness comes through service.

We live in a world chasing shortcuts, clout, and overnight success. But here's the truth: The person who serves with heart, consistency, and humility will outlast every hype trend. The work you do for others – that's what creates your legacy.

'The best way to find yourself is to lose yourself in the service of others.'

Mahatma Gandhi

If you're searching for a purpose, start by asking: 'How can I help?'

In a world that rewards shortcuts and celebrates hustle, doing the right thing is radical. But when you live with integrity, you stand out. You become unforgettable. Everyone's chasing 'the brand', but let me tell you something: When I started, I didn't know what a brand was. I just focused on being excellent, doing what was right, and putting in the work. That's what built Zed Nasheet.

Excellence is magnetic. Integrity leaves a mark. What you put out always finds its way back to you.

A couple of years ago, I ran an auction in Melbourne's southeast. The owner asked what I thought her property would sell for and I estimated between $720K and $760K. She looked stunned. Her ex-husband had secretly refinanced the house at $780K – a number she had no idea about.

Auction day came. The final bid hit $782K. I asked her, 'What would you like to do, Anne?'

She looked at me and said, 'Zed, you already know the answer. I can't sell. I owe the bank too much.'

So I did what felt right. I tore up the contract and didn't charge her a cent. No commission. No fees. No invoice. Just peace of mind – for her and for me. Because sometimes, success isn't in what you earn, it's in what you walk away from.

Not everyone will be happy when you start rising. Some will feel uncomfortable around your ambition, your vision, your energy. Your growth will challenge their comfort. And instead of saying. 'I'm inspired', they'll say, 'Who does he think he is?'

Here's what that really means: You're triggering something in them they haven't faced yet.

That's not your burden. Surround yourself with people who celebrate your shine, not those trying to dim it.

So, the most important question of all: Who do you want to be in this world? Not who your parents want you to be. Not who your friends expect you to be. Not who society says you should be.

Just you – at your most powerful, your most grounded, your most authentic.

You don't have to be perfect. You don't need all the answers. You just need the courage to begin, the integrity to do it right, and the heart to serve others along the way.

This is how you build a life that isn't just successful – but *significant.*

> **"YOU DON'T HAVE TO BE PERFECT. YOU DON'T NEED ALL THE ANSWERS. YOU JUST NEED THE COURAGE TO BEGIN, THE INTEGRITY TO DO IT RIGHT, AND THE HEART TO SERVE OTHERS ALONG THE WAY."**

FALL IN LOVE WITH REJECTION

Getting rejected on a daily basis might not seem fun, but think about it this way: If it were easy, everyone would be doing it. I always aimed at getting rejected at least 20 times a day from people walking past me. I knew that if I didn't speak to enough people, I wouldn't reach my goal by the end of the month or the year.

Keep repeating this to yourself: 'I love getting rejected', and make it your daily goal. Call me names, abuse me, hate or love me. I will still smile at you and ask if you are selling or buying. Respond to people's reactions with kindness. But bear in mind, if everyone said yes, there would be no need for salespeople.

The reason why you have a job is because people say *no* and *reject* you all the time. No matter how uncomfortable you get, someday you will look back and realise that your daily hustle changed your life for the better. Rejection provides you with the opportunity to differentiate yourself as an agent and rise to the top of the pack.

The Way I See It

If you want the rainbow, you have to put up with the rain. One day or day one – YOU DECIDE.

You should always be working on multiple deals at the same time because if one out of many goes down, you won't care. But if you only have one or two deals, and one of them doesn't work out, you'll have a serious problem. Keep your pipeline so full that you don't have the time to feel the impact of rejection because there are other clients to deal with.

Shift your focus from negative questions like, *How can I not get rejected?* to a simple reframe such as, *How can I fill my pipeline and get more leads?*

Similarly, change your thoughts from, *How can I increase the number of referrals I'm getting?* to something more purposeful, like, *How can I position myself on social media?* or, *How can I prospect more effectively?*

Once you get clear on that, you can deal with the cause and not merely the symptom.

OBJECTIONS ARE OPPORTUNITIES

The more successful you become, the more objections you'll encounter. It's a natural part of the sales process, and those who learn to navigate these challenges with ease are the ones who truly thrive. Most people give up too early and don't realise that every 'no' simply means 'not right now', and each rejection brings you one step closer to a 'yes'. Learning to handle objections with confidence builds your character, strengthens your resilience, and makes you a better problem-solver. Getting comfortable with objections every day will not only improve your skills but also make you a more solutions-focused and successful professional.

By embracing objections as opportunities rather than setbacks, you'll become a master at overcoming resistance and guiding prospects towards making decisions that benefit both them and you. Let's dive into how you can get comfortable handling objections and turn them into your greatest advantage.

ZED'S RITUALS FOR AN AGENT'S PERFECT DAY

The best part about being a real estate agent is that you are running a business within a business, and the benefits of being an agent include the freedom and flexibility of time this business gives you. You get to pick your own hours and have the freedom to work whenever or wherever you choose.

However, a lot of people take advantage of this freedom. Sleeping until 9:30 am, taking 30 minutes for a morning coffee, scrolling through social media platforms like Facebook, Instagram, Snapchat, or watching the news. Before you know it, it's 5:00 pm, an entire day has passed, and you have nothing valuable to offer to your marketplace. I'm sure many can relate to this.

There's a saying in business: 'If you're on time, you're late'. If you're 10 minutes early to an appointment, you're on time; and if you're late, it's unacceptable.

You've heard me say it before – you'll never change your life until you change something you do daily. The secret to your success is found in your daily routine. Routine and structure are what separate an okay agent from the top writer.

Plan and Execute

Plan your day in advance, plan your month, plan your year, and plan your five-year goals. Goals will give you a purpose to live, and what will separate you in your marketplace is consistency, persistence, and having structure in place. At the end of the day, you could learn all the secrets to success, but it's up to you to plan and take action.

'Success is a numbers game. Sales is a numbers game.'

The more people you talk to, the more opportunities you create for yourself.

Everyone is an opportunity in life. The question is: *Are you willing to create the opportunity?* ALL IT TAKES IS A SIMPLE QUESTION. The person who makes themselves uncomfortable daily is the person who will have all the necessary things they've always wanted. You have to make yourself uncomfortable on a daily basis so that tomorrow you can live the life you've dreamt of. I want you to solve your problems by becoming RICH.

You are who you surround yourself with. If you hang around five losers, you'll unconsciously join the party. Surround yourself with people who bring out the best in you and add value to your life.

If that's the lifestyle you're after, then this routine will definitely help you get there. But we have to walk first before we run. It all starts with small daily disciplines put into place on a daily basis.

Zed's Daily Blueprint: This Is How I Win My Day

If you want to perform at your highest level, it starts with how you spend your day – because the way you spend your day is the way you spend your life.

Here's my personal routine, hour by hour. You don't have to copy it exactly. The key is to build a rhythm that fuels *your* success, *your* energy, and *your* goals.

Disclaimer: I'm not a 5:00 am guy. I love my eight hours of sleep. I start at 7:00 am and finish strong. Work with your own energy clock, don't force someone else's hustle. Design a day that works *for you.*

7:00 AM – 8:00 AM

Wake Up with Purpose and Move Your Body

Start the day by feeding your energy – not your phone.

- Gym or walk + protein shake
- Stretch, hydrate, and get your body moving
- No scrolling. Fuel > distraction

The way you start your morning will determine how well you own your day.

8:00 AM – 9:00 AM

Morning Mindset Ritual

This is sacred. Prime your mind for performance. I call this hour my **mental conditioning** session.

- Gratitude practice
- Prayer or meditation
- Motivational videos (YouTube is gold)
- Audiobooks or a chapter of something inspiring
- Visualisation: Where are you headed? See it. Feel it.

Set your frequency. You don't attract what you want – you attract what you *are*.

9:00 AM – 10:00 AM

Daily Planning, Admin and Preparation

This is where you set up the chessboard for the rest of your day.

- Sync with your assistant (or your calendar)
- Review appointments + prep your materials
- Study your prospects like it's game day
- Research listings, areas, and comparable sales
- Roleplay key conversations or objections with a colleague
- Return every enquiry. Follow up. Keep your vendors updated.

Over-communicate. Over-deliver. Under-promise.
Clients will *never* complain that you're too involved.

10:00 AM – 11:00 AM

Mental Recharge and Community Connection

Take a break, but make it productive.

- Grab a coffee from your local café
- Say hello to familiar faces
- Take a walk, stretch, breathe

I once closed a $3M deal from a café chat. Opportunity is everywhere when you're present.

11:00 AM – 12:00 PM

Prospecting Power Hour

The rule is simple: **20 quality connections per day.** No excuses. No distractions. No fluff.

- Speak to past clients, new leads, referrals
- Text, call, voice note, DM – just connect
- Not sure what to say? Scripts are coming later in the book.

What you lack in skill, you make up for in volume. Keep dialling. Keep growing. Repetitions equal revenue.

12:00 PM – 6:30 PM

Appointments and Listings and Action

This is your money-making zone.

- Aim for **four appointments** in this block: appraisals, listings, showings
- If you're newer and don't have four? Use the time for more prospecting

- Keep your energy high, your game sharp, and your intention clear

Want better results? Work with purpose. Bring the energy. Own the outcome.

6:30 PM – 7:00 PM

Daily Wrap-Up and Reflection

Before you shut down:

- Review what you achieved
- Set your top three goals for tomorrow
- Send any final follow-ups or notes
- Tidy your workspace
- Shut off mentally

A powerful tomorrow starts with a clear today.

7:00 PM – 8:00 PM

Schedule your personal life *as seriously* as your business life.

- Eat with your family
- Ask better questions than 'How was your day?'
- Be present – not half-on-your-phone, half-in-the-room

Balance isn't found. It's scheduled.

8:00 PM – 9:00 PM

This hour is yours.

- Read something fun
- Be with your partner
- Pursue a hobby
- Journal or plan a future trip
- Laugh, chill, breathe

9:00 PM – 7:00 AM

Sleep is the ultimate productivity tool. Without it, you'll burn out. With it, you'll crush every goal.

- Seven to eight hours minimum
- No screens before bed
- Use sleep to reset your mindset

Success doesn't come from working 24/7. It comes from working intentionally – and resting like a pro. You don't need to be extreme. You just need to be consistent.

One power-packed day can change your momentum. Ten power-packed days can change your results. A few focused months can change your *life*.

Let this routine inspire you – but build your own version. The real flex? Living on your own terms with clarity, consistency, and confidence.

Find Yourself. Be Yourself.

Here's a truth most people forget: There is no one else on this planet exactly like you. That's not just a fluffy line – it's your superpower.

In a world where everyone is trying to fit in, the boldest thing you can do is stand out by being unapologetically YOU. When you stop pretending and start owning who you are – that's when things begin to shift.

The biggest mistake agents make is acting like someone they think the client wants. That's a fast track to burnout – and trust me, clients can smell inauthenticity from a mile away.

There's only one YOU. That's your most powerful point of difference. Don't hide it – highlight it.

Yesterday, I posted this on my story: If someone tells you 'you can't', they're showing you their limits, not yours.

Read that again.

People who try to put you in a box are usually stuck in one themselves. So let them doubt. Let them copy. Let them try to be someone else. You? Stay rooted in who you are.

Being yourself isn't just a feel-good quote – it's the most practical business strategy on the planet.

- People don't want perfect. They want real.
- People don't follow brands. They follow energy.
- People don't buy from robots. They buy from humans.

So stop trying to 'fit in'. You weren't born to blend. You were born to shine. And when you do that authentically, not only will you love your life – you'll love your business too.

> “
>
> IF SOMEONE TELLS YOU 'YOU CAN'T', THEY'RE SHOWING YOU THEIR LIMITS, NOT YOURS.
>
> ”

Embrace Your Story

I remember when I first started selling luxury real estate, I was scared and doubted myself a lot. Many people told me I wasn't good enough and that my style wouldn't work. They suggested I should change my style and approach. We are all human, and from time to time, we all doubt ourselves, regardless of how strong our mindset is. At one point, I thought maybe I should just fake it and tell them what they wanted to hear to get the job. I considered making up a story about coming from a rich background.

I will never forget an appraisal I did in Brighton – it was a $12M home, and the seller's son was really arrogant. During my presentation, I said, 'My dad owns private jets and doesn't talk to me because he wants me to take over his empire'. The reality is, my dad is retired. Sure, it felt good to put the arrogant kid in his place during the presentation, but deep down, I knew I wasn't telling the truth, and it didn't feel right. I thought if I told him the truth about my background, there's no way I would get the business. I was embarrassed to tell people I grew up in Pakistan, in a war zone, and started selling $300,000 properties in Hampton Park.

I was scared to tell people the truth. I wasn't embracing who I was and my approach. I was lying, and that's why my pitch wasn't coming out naturally. To be honest with you, I felt terrible inside during the presentation. I was hiding my identity, and my pitch wasn't authentic enough. Clients could feel it, but I didn't feel right about it. It wasn't about them; it was about me. I was embarrassed about where I had come from, and I seriously thought I would lose clients by sharing my story.

The reality is, we all have those fears, and we doubt ourselves when dealing with people because we want their business. But I can guarantee you now, I get 50 times more business when I share my story and am authentic and genuine in my approach. Your clients can feel your enthusiasm and your passion when it comes from the bottom of your heart.

Embrace Your Journey

Ever since I embraced my story and my family's story, people are connecting with me all over social media because they have similar journeys, and they're embracing it. It's giving people hope that there's room for growth. It's better to be you than to pretend to be somebody you are not.

Unlock Your Full Potential

The average person develops only 10 percent of their mental abilities. Compared to what we should or need to be, we are only half awake. We are making use of only a small part of our physical and mental resources. We live life with fear and live within our limits. You and I have such abilities, so don't waste a second worrying about not being like other people. You are something new in this world. Never before, since the beginning of time, has anyone ever looked like you – and they never will.

You need to be you, with all your faults and limitations. Don't be ashamed of where you've come from.

A favourite quote from Douglas Malloch, American poet, journalist and editor, keeps me going on a daily basis: 'Be a bush if you can't be a tree. If you can't be a bush, be a bit of the grass. We can't all be captains, we've got to be crew. There's something for all of us here. If you can't be a highway, then just be a trail. If you can't be the sun, be a star. It isn't by size that you win or fail – be the best of whatever you are!'

Let's not copy others. Let's find ourselves and be the best version of ourselves.

Today is Going to Be the Best Day Ever

If It's Not in Your Schedule, It Doesn't Exist

You forget your purpose and your mission. If we can do the right things in the morning, then your day flows. Imagine for 280 days out of 365 days you designed your whole year – you'd know exactly what you're aiming for and where you're going. This can apply not just to work, but to everything you do, including what you eat.

Encourage Yourself

Say to yourself, 'This is going to be the best day ever'. Whether it's handling objections, role-playing, dealing with cold clients, or following up with previous ones, practise your pitch with cold leads and then follow up with the hot ones.

Imagine if You Designed Your Day

Imagine if you designed your day and your next 280 days were spent prospecting. When you do these things, you have the power.

If you do this, your week will be packed. You'll be negotiating, closing, and enjoying it, and there won't be any time left for pitching or looking at other listings.

Let Me Say This Again

If it's not in your schedule, it doesn't exist. If you design your schedule, you win. This is your time. I'm asking you to step up and start having more perfect days. Create your schedule, follow the routine, and celebrate your wins.

Real Estate is a Sport: Train Hard, Create Your Own Luck

Real estate is a sport. The more you practise, the better you become at it – except no one is going to tell you what kind of sport it is until the bell rings. When you start to sell more and have your weekly and monthly goals written down, it becomes clear that what you put out is what you will receive.

There are no shortcuts to selling more – just hard work. The more people you speak to, the more opportunities you create. There is no such thing as luck – luck is when preparation meets opportunity. If you work harder, you typically have better preparation. Therefore, you are in a better position when the opportunity arrives.

I've had a lot of help from great people along the way, and for that, I'm grateful. That being said, the way I see it, I choose to be luckier. You make your own luck. Not only that, but I'm always in control of the one thing that can make more: working my butt off.

If you want to do great things, you better be willing to hustle, grind, and work for what you want. There are seven days in a week, not five. You have to be persistent and consistent with this mindset on a daily basis in order to get to your end goal.

Where Risk Creates Wealth

I love selling high-end homes. The luxury market has a certain energy that excites me. But you know what else gets me fired up? Selling development sites to investors. Working with developers. Watching people take a risk on raw land or a project – and helping them turn that into real, lasting wealth.

There's something powerful about being part of someone's journey to financial freedom. When the deal settles, and I know I've played a role in creating a better future for that person or family... nothing beats that.

But here's the truth: there's no freedom without risk.

Risk Is Everywhere – You Just Learn to Dance With It

Think about it. The day you were born, there was risk. The day you got married, there was risk. The day you started your business, had a kid, bought your first home – all risk.

People talk about risk like it's something to be feared. I see it as the price of entry for a better life.

Because nothing in life that's worth having comes without it. If financial freedom were easy – if wealth creation came without stress, sacrifice, or sleepless nights – everyone would have it. But they don't. And that's what separates those who dream… from those who decide.

Here's something I've learned: You must be willing to do the things others avoid, so that tomorrow, you can have the life others only wish for.

That might mean making 50 calls when everyone else stops at 10 or following up when others give up. Attending inspections, auctions, events – rain or shine. Taking a risk on a deal that your gut tells you is right, even if your fear says 'wait'.

This isn't about gambling. It's about believing – in yourself, in the vision, in the work. You don't get financial freedom by chance. You get it by choice. You're one decision away from a completely different life. Don't wait for the perfect moment, the perfect market, or the perfect deal. They don't exist.

The ones who win are the ones who move anyway. They bet on themselves, they back their ideas, and they believe the risk is worth the reward. So ask yourself: Are you building someone else's dream? Or are you ready to start building your own? Because financial freedom? It's not a fantasy.

It's a choice. And the power to make that choice… is already in your hands.

"

YOU'RE ONE DECISION AWAY FROM A COMPLETELY DIFFERENT LIFE. DON'T WAIT FOR THE PERFECT MOMENT, THE PERFECT MARKET, OR THE PERFECT DEAL. THEY DON'T EXIST.

"

THE RIGHT MINDSET

If you want to win – really win – in life, business, and everything in between, it all starts with your mindset. The right mindset is not just something you stumble into. It's something you build, nurture, and protect like it's your greatest asset – because it is.

No matter your background, your bank account, or what your teacher told you in school, this truth stands strong:

Your mindset will either unlock your greatness or keep you locked in your limitations.

And the best part? You get to choose which one it is.

Let me walk you through the mental frameworks that have shaped my own journey – from being just another agent trying to make it… to building an empire, closing eight-figure deals, and helping thousands of people do the same.

1. Self-Trust Mindset

Greatness starts with a conversation between you and the person in the mirror. Before you expect anyone else to believe in you, you must believe in yourself. Full stop. Self-trust is the foundation of all confidence. When you trust your instincts, your decisions, and your ability to figure it out – there's nothing you can't do. Even when it's hard. Even when no one's clapping yet. Even when the outcome isn't guaranteed.

2. Goal-Setting Mindset

Don't drift through life – design it. Clarity is power. Set clear goals. Map out your outcomes. Know what success looks like for you, and then reverse-engineer the steps to get there.

Without goals, you're just busy. With goals, you're dangerous.

3. Patient Mindset

We live in a world addicted to instant gratification. Real success takes time, consistency, and the patience to play the long game. Hustle today. Harvest tomorrow. Trust the process and stay committed. Most people quit three metres from gold – don't let that be you.

4. Courageous Mindset

Fear is normal. Doubt is human. But courage is a choice. Every successful person you admire faced fear and pushed through it.

Courage isn't the absence of fear – it's doing it despite the fear. Whether it's a cold call, a bold business move, or a big life decision, step up and lean in.

That's where your next level lives.

5. Focused Mindset

Distractions are the enemy of dreams. Every notification, every excuse, every concern over what others are doing is a moment stolen from your purpose.

Laser focus on your goals. Protect your energy. And stop scrolling – it's someone else's highlight reel, not your reality.

6. Positive Mindset

Your attitude sets your altitude. Positivity isn't about ignoring problems. It's about choosing to face them with strength and the belief that you can overcome them. It's about waking up and saying: 'Today, I'm going to win. I don't know how yet, but I will'.

That belief is how champions are made.

7. Learning Mindset

The most dangerous words in business: 'I already know that'. Stay a student. Stay humble. Stay hungry.

Every expert was once a beginner, and every beginner becomes a master through learning, trial, error, and more learning. Read books. Watch people smarter than you. Invest in mentorship. Learn something new every single day.

Believe You Are Worthy

This one's big. If you don't believe you're worthy of happiness, of success, of wealth – you'll sabotage it before it even shows up. You must truly believe that you are worthy of abundance. That you deserve love, joy, money, peace, and freedom. Because you do.

Want to attract wealth? Start by believing you're worthy of it. And while you're at it:

- Focus on what you already have.
- Stop comparing.
- Let go of jealousy – it drains your power.
- Respect money. Study money. And yes – give money away.

You'll discover something powerful: money flows where it's respected, not where it's worshipped.

The Truth: Anyone Can

Let me break it down for you. Anyone can become wealthy. Anyone can become independent. Anyone can build a business. Anyone can turn their life around.

But very few do. Why? Because most people are too busy chasing shortcuts instead of building skills. They jump in, struggle, and wonder why it's not working.

Don't do that.

Follow proven systems. Learn from people who've walked the path. Plug into mentors, courses, Zed Talks – anything that gives you an edge. That's how you collapse time.

I've made it my mission to help as many people as I can rise to their true greatness. And I hope this chapter has helped move you one step closer to yours.

You don't need permission. You just need the right mindset.

Believe You Are Worthy of Happiness

Part of attracting wealth requires that you believe you are worthy of happiness. Focus on what you have right now. End the cycle of learned helplessness. Purge jealousies. Respect the power of money. Study wealth. And give money away.

The truth is, there's no such thing as luck. It's just another excuse. Nothing happens without a cause.

HOW YOU BECOME AN INFLUENCE

There is only one of you that looks like you in the world. You are special and unique – remember that.

Those who influence dominate in life. They dominate their environment, and people respect them. Don't confuse fame with influence. Not everyone who is influential is popular, but they are impactful. Jesus and the messengers were influential, not popular.

They made a difference and had an impact on people's lives.

You Were Born to Influence

You don't need to live long to influence the planet. Your presence and your actions can leave a lasting impact.

6P RULES FOR LIFE

1. **PLAN** everything in your life, no matter what. Plan and get unexpected surprises. Set and plan your goals daily.
2. **PREPARE** for whatever you do in life. Ask yourself: *How much time do I need?* and *How much effort am I putting into my business?*
3. **PRACTISE** – practise the skills you need in life and business. Apply the discipline from sports into your work, whether it's prospecting, phone calls, or door knocking.
4. **PERFORM** – when negotiating for a property or in a listing presentation, treat it like a performance. Give it your all, and deliver with excellence.
5. **PRODUCE** – what you perform is what you produce. Your actions lead to your results.
6. **PARTY** – celebrate your success based on the results you have produced. Recognise and enjoy your achievements along the way.

Be You and Own It!

'I'd rather be hated for who I am, than be loved for who I am not'.

Kurt Cobain

You will never win in life by trying to be someone you're not. You cannot live the life of your dreams by settling for someone else's idea of what you should be doing. You will never be happy if you change who you are to fit in. Until you accept and embrace who you are, you are destined to live a life that is merely a fraction of your potential.

It is impossible to be genuinely happy when you are not your genuine self. If you're different, be different and take pride in it! If someone doesn't like it, even if most people don't like it, why care? Those aren't the people for you.

The right people will show up when the real you comes out. There will always be someone prettier, always someone smarter, but there will never be another you.

Honestly, you will never be hated by the right people for being real. Being yourself is the greatest filter you can ever use. It instantly clears out all the people who don't belong with you and at the same time, reveals those who do.

The only problem is that people are often hated when they're real and loved when they're fake. The ones who do this are fake themselves.

So, who do you want to attract?

Be yourself, and I promise you, eventually, you will attract the right people. Be yourself, no matter what has happened to you and no matter who has hurt you. Be kind. If you can, life will turn out far greater than you ever thought possible. If you don't, life will be painful.

Living with a mask on, trying to fit in, and altering yourself may cause others to like you, but it will not make you feel complete or happy.

> **Repeat to yourself every day:**
> 'I am different, and that is why I win. I am unique, and that is why I am great. I am unlike anyone else on this planet. I am grateful for who I am, and I am grateful for who I am becoming. I am committed to being myself and speaking my truth at all times. I know that this is the only way for the right people to show up in my life. Those who are meant for me will love and support me, being real with the real me. I will stand tall and stay strong in my purpose, and in everything that matters to me.'

I Love Getting No

Chase after a no, not a yes. And the more Nos you get, the closer you get to a YES. Can you imagine thriving off a No rather than a Yes?

Your new task is to get 50 Nos on a daily basis, and when you finally get a Yes, it will feel like a triumph and boost your confidence manifold.

Safe to say, **I LOVE GETTING A NO.**

Who Knows You Wins: Facing Fear to Stand Out

I still remember the day I started making property videos. It was 1.20 pm on a public holiday – Australia Day, 26th January. Social media wasn't big in 2010; I had a MySpace account and Messenger – the good old days. I was very new to real estate and could see how serious the agents were in the area – ties all the way up, clean shaven, suits on, no creativity, no innovation. Pen and paper at open homes, and it would take them three days to respond to an enquiry.

I saw a big opportunity and asked myself how I could be more creative and what change I could bring to the industry. That's when the new iPhone was in fashion, and YouTube videos were becoming more popular. I came up with property videos that started out with the usual intro and outro like others had done in the past, but it didn't take me far. Then I added a bit of cheesiness – dressing up in Superman, Spider-Man, and Super Mario outfits, even doing a rap video to sell a $3 million listing just to break into the marketplace.

Within a couple of months, it was the talk of the town. Hundreds of people started sharing it. That's when I realised the power of videos. I learned that in business, it's not about who you know; it's about who knows you.

“

**I LEARNED THAT IN BUSINESS,
IT'S NOT ABOUT WHO YOU KNOW;
IT'S ABOUT WHO KNOWS YOU.**

”

Fear and Courage in Action

Did I fear while doing those videos? I sure did. I didn't know how my clients would react. People are already so stressed and nervous about buying a home – the last thing they want is to deal with another salesperson. Remember, customers buy YOU first before they buy your product.

Buying real estate should be memorable and exciting. Did my competition make fun of it? Yes, they sure did. Did most of my friends laugh at it? They sure did. They made fun of my accent, too. Even viewers gave me hate, but guess what? They all talked about me and spread my name by word of mouth – good or bad.

Did I make mistakes? Of course, I did. But no one gets out of life without making mistakes. We learn far more from failure than from success. They laughed at me because I was different, and I laugh now because they're all the same.

You may not be able to control every situation and its outcome, but you can control your attitude and how you deal with it.

If you kill the fear inside you, the fear outside will do no harm. You need to kill the enemy within first. It's all about self-talk – the thoughts in your head and what you feed your mind. Repeat to yourself, 'This is your life, and you're entitled to live it the way you want. Nothing or no one will come in between you and your goals'.

People's opinions don't pay your bills. Let your fear drive you like nothing else. Let the fears in you be the fuel that propels you towards greatness.

The life I've built for myself – Z. Real Estate, Zed Media, Zlogs on my YouTube channel, my beautiful home, my investment properties, my amazing cars I get to enjoy on beautiful days, and my future Z. TOWER – looks very different from the day I started believing in myself and stopped worrying about what others had to say about me.

I will never forget the days when I was broke, couldn't afford to pay my phone bill, had no fuel in my car, was emotional, lost, and surrounded by negative energy. But I didn't listen to anyone but myself.

Today, every deal I make, every property I sell, seven days of hard work with no days off for 60 days straight. I work to distance myself as far as I can from those past experiences. It was my self-belief and discipline that got me to where I am today.

Motivation Through Struggle

By now, you've figured out that my biggest motivation in life is the background I come from – Afghanistan, one of the poorest countries in the world, in constant war for 50 years. I want to provide my parents with financial freedom after all they've been through. I support orphans and people who have lost loved ones in the war, helping them through education and financial freedom so they can put food on the table.

Overcoming Fear to Achieve Greatness

Do not let anyone put fear inside your head and scare you into thinking it's not possible. Your motivation is what will drive you to achieve anything you've always wanted. You've got to focus on you, because you sell you to you. It takes courage to act and to start over again every day. Push yourself every day, and never take it personally when people reject you or put you down.

The Power of Yes: Turning Challenges into Opportunities and Zelling More

It's easy to say no. It's easy to make excuses about why you can't close a deal. It's much easier to focus on what could go wrong or the immediate challenges. But none of that stopped me from prospecting daily. I kept building myself until I created enough opportunities.

I'm the *Yes Man* from the movie with Jim Carrey. I've said yes to many things: taking on listings that have been sitting on the market for ages, creating funny property videos, representing clients who were almost impossible to deal with, opening an office in the middle of lockdown, investing in property during the riskiest times, and starting a company with my brother Maseeh, who had no real estate experience. The list goes on. Very rarely do you hear me say no. In fact, it's almost never.

I sell more because I say yes when others would say no. I keep moving a client forward until the deal is done. Saying yes to every opportunity was my way of believing in myself and proving I was the best – even when I wasn't. I've also learned that quickly flipping negatives into positives helps you close deals faster and more frequently.

Sometimes, this is as simple as asking yourself, 'Is this negative really even a negative?' For example, if I'm selling a house with no land – or let's say a small land size – I'll push this as a positive to a client who is rarely home or dislikes gardening. Why pay extra for a home with more land that you don't have time to maintain?

I talk about the 80 percent positive and 20 percent negative rule. Take the time to think about the usual objections you hear in your area of sales – it's likely you'll encounter the same ones repeatedly. How can you show clients that this isn't really a negative? How can you turn this around? Anticipating objections and immediately reframing them as positives will result in you Zelling more.

Saying yes = Zelling More.

Don't be afraid to say yes, even if you're unsure what you're doing or where to start. You'd be surprised how many salespeople say no to opportunities simply because stepping into uncharted territory makes them uncomfortable. Saying yes gives you an enormous advantage over your competition.

I understand how terrifying it can be to say yes. I've said yes to many opportunities, and those that scared me the most often turned out to be the most rewarding – both financially and emotionally. Don't forget, you have the power to figure things out. And if someone thinks you're crazy for saying yes, even better – they don't have the courage to do what you're doing.

Say yes to opportunities so you have plenty of prospects to work with. Persuade clients to say yes to making purchases. Say yes to taking risks. When you're asked to do something new or completely foreign, even if you have no idea how to do it, say yes and trust yourself to figure it out later. This automatically puts you ahead of every salesperson who said no.

There will always be objections to almost every single sale. The goal is to turn those negatives into positives.

The Foundation of a Winner

In real estate, just like in life, success starts with the right foundation – not just in property, but in mindset, habits, and who you choose to surround yourself with.

If you want to grow, thrive, and dominate – whether as an agent, investor, or entrepreneur – you need to align with those who believe in building more. People who think big, who challenge you, who push you forward when you're tired and hold you accountable when you're slacking. These are the people who help you expand, not shrink.

Real growth doesn't happen in comfort. Staying stuck at the bottom is easy – it requires no effort, no courage, no discomfort. But if you want to reach the top in this business, you'll need to climb. That means facing rejection, pushing through self-doubt, and showing up every single day – especially when no one's watching.

Your biggest obstacle will always be yourself. Not the competition. Not the market. Not the interest rates. It's your own fear. Your own hesitation. Your own belief that maybe you're not enough.

But here's the truth: your past does not define your future. Maybe you've made mistakes. Missed deals. Lacked discipline. That was then. Today is new. Right now, you have the chance to rewrite the story – brick by brick, deal by deal, step by step.

Stop wasting energy on doubt, excuses, or complaining. Use it to move forward. To take the next step. To build the future you know you're capable of. Let go of past failures – they're lessons, not life sentences. Stop playing small. The world doesn't need more people playing it safe. It needs more leaders, more doers, more dreamers willing to put in the work.

“

WHEN WE CHANGE OUR THOUGHTS,
WE CAN CHANGE WHAT WE ACHIEVE.

”

THINK BIGGER, EARN BIGGER: THE POWER OF A MILLION DOLLAR MINDSET

I'm successful beyond my wildest dreams because of my million dollar mindset.

The truth is, we can't achieve anything without the right mindset. If you desire more than just basic enjoyment and free time, let's explore the concept of mindset and its importance.

Our mindsets are made up of the beliefs and attitudes that help us understand the world and our place in it. Mindsets are flexible and can change over time. So, if you currently have a negative or defeatist mindset, my aim is to help you change it.

Put simply, when we change our thoughts, we can change what we achieve.

Having a mindset geared for success is all about taking yourself to the next level. You don't have to be in the luxury real estate business to apply this advice because aiming high can work in any situation where you're trying to reach a common goal, whether it's sealing a deal with a handshake or finalising a complex contract at a big company.

The key rules for having a success-oriented mindset are to always aim for something bigger and better than what you have now, and be ready to put in the work to make it happen.

In the early days of Z. Real Estate, when I hadn't ZOLD much luxury real estate in Brighton, I had to negotiate a deal where the sellers wanted $5.5 million for their home, but the buyer was stuck at $5.45 million. Although $5.5 million was a fair price, I panicked over the $50,000 difference. I felt tempted to give in and lower my commission by $50,000 to close the deal quickly. But I realised that giving in wouldn't help me grow as an agent in the long run.

While compromise can be necessary at times, in this case, because of my mindset, lowering my commission was the wrong move. I let my fear of losing the sale get to me, stopping me from fighting for the right price. I needed to separate my emotions from the situation and think logically.

I looked at my past successes and failures objectively and realised that I had achieved more successes than failures. This was a fact, not just a feeling. I believed that if I continued to work hard and smart, I would have many successful deals in my career. I focused on building a reputation as someone who fights for what's right, not someone who gives in easily. This mindset shift set me on the path to success.

With my new mindset, I went back to the buyer and stood firm on the seller's final price. I emphasised the value of the property. I educated the buyer. I spoke 80 percent positive and 20 percent negative about the home so the buyers could think I'm on their side, as nothing in life is perfect and nothing will ever be perfect. In the end, I closed the deal at $5.5 million, with the buyer going up by $50,000. The million-dollar mindset worked, and it helped me identify serious buyers from those looking for a bargain.

For me, the million dollar mindset is about having a positive attitude, using successful strategies, and having a personal philosophy focused on winning with integrity. This mindset isn't just about business; it can transform your entire life. By embracing this mindset, I've achieved wealth beyond my expectations, not just financial riches.

The Finish Line Mindset: Keep Climbing, Keep Winning

What's your great dream? A glamorous wedding? A house on the beach? Climbing Mount Everest? Don't be afraid to dream bigger.

Big goals can't be accomplished overnight. What are the small steps you need to take to get there? Which action can you take today that will move you closer to your dream? Nothing is insurmountable when broken down into small, achievable tasks.

Of course, there will be times when you feel like giving up – when the climb seems too steep, the clouds too dark, and the disappointment too heavy to bear. When you think, 'I can't go any further. I can't do any more. I've plateaued, I've reached my limit, and the only way from here is down', know this: you're not alone.

Even the most successful people I know have doubts. When you feel like giving up, close your eyes and visualise yourself crossing the finish line. Picture yourself achieving your dream. The secret is to keep the finish line in mind – and don't stop when you get there. The most successful people don't just stop at the finish line; they set their sights on the next challenge.

Remember, your dreams are the fuel for your journey. Embrace them, pursue them, and never let them go.

Steps to Get Out of Your Comfort Zone and Be Your True Self

How do you find and express the real you? I know it sounds simple, but for a lot of people, it's not. Don't despair. You can do it in four easy steps:

1. Look Inside.

In today's society, with everyone on social media trying to prove how happy and accomplished they are, life can sometimes feel like a giant competition – but it's not. On some level, it is a race, yes, but it's only a race against yourself.

You are your own competition. We all start and end the race alone, and that's a beautiful thing if you give it some thought. And one of the first rules of business is to know your competition, which in this case means knowing yourself.

How would you describe yourself? Are you funny? Empathetic? Do you have an interesting talent? Can you juggle, read palms, or perform sleight of hand? Are you an amazing cha-cha dancer? Do you play sports? Whatever it is, embrace it and make it your strength. Capitalise on it. Don't be afraid to bring out your box of tricks, make them stronger, and show them off. It will make others fall in love with the real you.

2. Get Over What Other People Think.

Other people's opinions and thoughts don't have to be your reality. Let go of trying to please everyone or live up to anyone else's expectations. It just doesn't work, and that's a proven fact.

If you're not true to yourself and you try to change for others, you'll only grow sad because no matter how much approval you gain, you won't approve of yourself. You are the one you need to make happy. Be yourself; everyone else is already taken.

When you embrace your authenticity, others will feel comfortable around you and will naturally gravitate towards you. It might take time, but it's worth the wait.

I know successful people who hide their true selves, and I see how empty their success feels because it isn't really theirs – it's borrowed or copied from someone else.

Remember there's only one of you that looks like you out of eight billion people, you are already special and amazing, embrace yourself and share yourself with the world in an honest way and watch the magic in it. You were born to be you. Don't let anyone tell you otherwise.

3. Know What Fuels Your Engine.

What gives you energy? What fuels your passion and drives you to get out of bed every day?

4. Embrace Your Amazingness.

Use this energy to give you fuel and you need to love yourself before others love you, if you don't love and respect yourself how do you expect others to. Once you realise how amazing you are, everyone else will too. Confidence is attractive not cockiness but confidence. When you fully embrace your unique qualities, you'll not only find joy but also inspire others to do the same.

Start today. Look inside, let go of outside expectations, and shine as the authentic version of yourself. Joy is eternal, and it begins with you.

The Power of Looking Good: Boost Your Confidence and Sales

When you look good, you feel good. And when you look and feel good, it helps your clients feel great about themselves, too. It's always a great feeling when someone compliments you, saying you look sharp. You want your clients to remember you for how polished you appear, as your appearance plays a significant role in your success. Remember, while God judges the inside, people judge the outside. Your first impression is often your lasting one.

I always advise new salespeople to set aside five percent of each commission cheque for their wardrobe and grooming. This small investment can have a big impact on your sales. While some books suggest saving for retirement, I believe enhancing your appearance today can lead to greater rewards in the future. Let's explore how you can use this money effectively.

Tailored Suits for a Stronger Image

In real estate, your appearance speaks volumes. A big mistake I see, especially with new agents, is buying clothes off the rack without having them tailored. Personally, I like my clothes fitted, but everyone has their preference – whether it's more fitted or a bit looser. The key is that your clothes should be altered to flatter your body and highlight your strengths. If you've ever looked behind a store mannequin, you've probably noticed that it's always pinned and adjusted to perfection. That's exactly how your clothes should fit: tailored to your shape, not just purchased and worn as-is.

When you're in a business like real estate, where you're meeting clients face-to-face all the time, your clothes should always make you look your best. That's why having a good tailor is essential. I personally get all my shirts and suits adjusted. I buy pants at their raw length and have them hemmed to my exact size. I'm fortunate that my mum helps with most of my tailoring, but even if you don't have someone in your family who's good with a needle, it's worth finding an expert tailor.

Tailoring doesn't have to break the bank. For me, it usually costs around $20 per shirt and $50 per suit. If you're trying to save, you might have an aunt, uncle, or friend who can help you cut costs without sacrificing quality. But no matter what, I believe every professional, whether you're a man or woman in real estate, should invest in tailoring. It's a small cost that makes a huge difference in how you look and feel – and it can help you stand out in a competitive market.

Here's a tip: You don't need to wear expensive, branded clothes to look good. It's not about the price; it's about how you wear it that makes you shine. With the right expertise, a $300 suit can look just like a $2,000 one.

The Impact of Well-Polished Shoes

I'll never forget an open inspection in Carlton, Melbourne. I was showing a property to a lawyer who looked absolutely sharp from head to toe. What stood out to me the most was how polished his shoes were. I asked him how he kept them so pristine, and he told me, 'I try to keep everything polished and neat'. That stuck with me. Every step he took, I couldn't help but notice how perfect his shoes looked. It may sound odd, but his attention to detail left a lasting impression.

Everyone notices your shoes. Trust me, what's on your feet can either elevate your outfit or take away from it. You want your shoes to make a positive impression with every step you take.

The Value of Investing in a Watch

If there's one thing I've invested in, it's watches. Along with cars, they've become a personal collection. I've got a watch for every occasion – casual ones for everyday wear and business watches to match my suits. I often get compliments on them, with people asking where I got them. A nice watch is more than just an accessory – it's a statement. It's something everyone notices, often even more than a wedding band.

If you can't afford a luxury watch today, save up for one. Find a picture of your dream watch and keep it in your goals list or on your bedroom wall. A watch is like a billboard, subtly communicating success and style. And for women, I love seeing a bold, oversized watch – it sends a powerful message.

A watch can be sentimental too. I didn't have my grandfather's watch, but I've built my own collection. You don't need a huge collection, but owning a quality watch – whether new or used – can make a strong impression. It becomes part of your identity, like an old friend that's with you through the highs and lows.

The Power of a Smile

"

THERE'S NOTHING MORE ATTRACTIVE THAN A SMILE.

"

As a kid, I struggled with my teeth. I never had straight teeth, and we couldn't afford braces, so I visited countless dentists. I was always shy about my smile and avoided showing it, especially in photos. Any chance I had, I'd hide my smile. But the best investment I've ever made – more than real estate or any other asset – was in veneers and crowns. I told my dentist to give me the best smile, no matter the cost. Now, I smile everywhere I go, and I even smile at myself in the mirror to boost my energy. It's amazing how much a smile can uplift your mood.

There's nothing more attractive than a smile. If your teeth are yellow, whiten them! A smile draws people in, while a scowl pushes them away. Smiling not only makes you look more confident but also opens doors to more opportunities. It's a simple truth. People are naturally attracted to those who smile. I learned this the hard way – early in my career, I was awkward in interviews, and I looked nervous and serious on camera. But over time, I realised how powerful a smile can be. Now, I smile more in interviews, and I see the difference. My phone rings more, my social media grows, and people find me approachable.

Smiling has incredible health benefits too. It reduces stress, boosts your immune system, and lowers your blood pressure. Plus, it releases serotonin and endorphins – nature's feel-good chemicals. Smiling even gives you a natural facelift by lifting the muscles in your face. It's like a free, no-surgery facelift! Try it right now: smile big, hold it, and notice how it lifts your mood. I bet you feel better already. Keep smiling for a week and see how it improves everything.

When I'm well-groomed, with a fresh tan, a great suit, a favourite watch, and, of course, a big smile, I feel like I can conquer the world. How you look directly impacts how you feel, and how you feel impacts your performance. Whether you're a telephone operator or a CEO, if you feel good about your appearance, you'll feel more positive about yourself, and that confidence will show in everything you do.

A first impression happens in the blink of an eye. Never underestimate its power. Presentation is something we can control, and how we present ourselves to the world is important. If you wrap yourself up nicely, like a present, you're giving the best version of yourself to the world. Make your appearance a ritual of self-love and watch how it transforms your life. You'll never look back.

Mastering Confidence, Connection, and Performance

While a good attitude and confidence are important to have, none of that matters if you don't put these factors into play on the job. When I'm competing to list a home, I might be competing against up to four other agents, so it's crucial that my confidence is on point and that my message is consistent. These competitive situations usually happen when an elderly person passes away and the trust or family is selling off the property.

The tone of my pitch will vary based on the personality of whomever I meet. The way I address an executor might be entirely different from how I'd speak with an owner's grandchild, but the content of my message doesn't change. Also, I'm confirming that with whomever I speak, we're of the same tribe and that I belong there. But before I even go into the appointment, I reflect on everything the potential seller needs to hear, and then it's my duty to hit every talking point once I'm in front of him or her.

When I have a listing appointment, I do my best. It's a performance. Every day we get up, we are performing at something or for a specific task. It doesn't matter if you're in real estate or not – you could be a personal trainer, and this could apply to you. You can choose to be a good performer or a great performer. It's like a sport. I love cricket, and when I walk through a house, I imagine I'm the best player there is. I'm on the field waiting for the bowler to bowl so I can hit it for six runs. The same thing applies in real estate – I'm performing because it's a performance.

As I read the room, first, I take the temperature of the client. I figure out what kind of person they are by the questions I ask. Within a few minutes of finding out who they are, I adjust my approach accordingly. I become who they want and need me to be... Depending on the client, I might have to be a footy fan, even though I don't watch it, but we can pretend to like it, right? I turn into a best friend, a comedian – sometimes I get asked about my religious beliefs or what I believe in, and my response is, 'What do you want me to be today?' I do whatever it takes to get the deal done.

After I've figured out what the seller is like and the best way to connect with them, I go into those talking points. The first thing I stress is that we have a huge team; it's not just me. I emphasise that we don't have over 20 offices and 600 people working for us like the majority of the big organisations – we are a small boutique agency that specialises in quality rather than quantity. I always get asked if I will be the agent running the campaign, and I always do.

Anyway, I tell the seller that they're going to get me zelling their property. I state this reality many different times and ways. (Did you notice?) Studies show the average person must hear something at least seven times before committing that piece of information to fact. We remember because of repetition, and the more someone hears a specific detail or feature, the more likely they are to believe it. Advertisers use this trick extensively. You know how sometimes you'll watch a streaming show?

Say it once, say it twice, but saying it seven times is nice.

I make sure the seller understands they're going to get my phone number so they can call me any time. There's no reason I'd ever be unreachable for more than a few minutes – I live and die by my phone. I literally dive on my phone when it rings because it could be money calling.

I don't have an ego about not selling my listings myself. I want to be in the mix. I get those listings because I'm dying to be the one who presents them to a buyer because no one will have done their homework like me. If a seller signs with me, they get me. End of story.

I like to remind potential sellers, 'You're paying me a lot of money for my service, so you're damn well going to get me. You deserve my full attention'. That's so important to stress... and wouldn't be believable if not delivered with confidence.

Why Do I Do This?

It's not because clients are paying me too much – they aren't. I know my worth. Instead, I'm stressing the value of my services. If they pay less, they get less. Saying the quiet part out loud actually builds trust because I'm acknowledging to the seller that I know – and will handle – my responsibilities.

Specifically telling sellers I'm expensive is a baller move that works.

Look at it this way: Do you want to get surgery from a plastic surgeon who boasts about having the lowest prices, or will you be more confident with the doctor who is unapologetic about their fees? There are places you just do not want to cut corners, and real estate is one of them.

Embracing Small Joys for Greater Success

I think it's a bit crazy when someone says they will stop buying their daily coffee to save money. We all need little treats to feel good about our hard work. If you cut out things that make you happy, you're setting yourself up to fail.

I'm surprised by people who never take a break. Taking holidays is common in many places to stay healthy, have a good family life, and work better. A study found that men who didn't take holidays for five years were more likely to have heart problems. Not taking time off is bad for your health and your work.

Success should feel good, right? I like to have small treats to stay motivated. Don't deny yourself joy; give yourself more! These treats can help you make more money. You've probably heard of a bucket list, right? It's a list of things you want to do before you die. That's cool, but you can also do things now to feel successful.

Let's call it Zed's Fun List. These are things that make you say, 'I'm treating myself today!'

1. **Learn something new:** What do you love? What do you want to learn? Cooking? Painting? Singing? Playing an instrument? Sign up to learn it! Your mind and business will benefit.
2. **Treat yourself:** Going on a shopping spree is fun. Walk around in new clothes or cool sunglasses and see how special you feel. You'll feel more confident.
3. **Eat at a fancy restaurant:** I love to take my loved ones out to eat at nice places. Yum! I may save money on lunch, but dinner is on me!
4. **Have a party:** Be a host and shine. Get help with cooking and hosting. I prefer hiring a chef so I can focus on other things.

5. **Stay at a fancy hotel:** Treat yourself to a nice hotel room in your town for a fancy night away. It's fun, and you'll save on expensive flights.

Trust Your Feelings and Find Job Satisfaction

Many people stay in jobs that don't motivate them. I'm not saying you should quit right away if you don't like your job. But if you're unhappy, trust your gut and look for something that makes you happy. Work takes up too much time for you to be miserable. If you're unhappy or don't care, it will affect your whole life, and that's hard to deal with. If something feels wrong, it probably is. It might be time to find a new job that inspires you every day in the long run.

If you're a strong and motivated salesperson, you can sell anything. And when you're not selling, you're losing money. Learning to be efficient is a lifestyle. If you're unhappy in your job, you have to trust your instincts and search for something that will fulfil you.

Stand Up for Yourself: How to Get What You Deserve

The lesson here is that it's okay to go after what you want, as long as you can show you deserve it. Whether it's a raise, stock options, a promotion, or more creative freedom, if you don't ask, you won't get it. Don't always wait for your boss to see your worth. Take the time to list your strengths and what you've done for the company, then approach your boss in a smart and polite way. Don't demand, don't beg, and don't criticise your co-workers. Focus on yourself and explain why you should get what you need to be happy and appreciated in your job.

Follow Your Feelings, Work Hard, and Make Clear Plans

When you find the perfect job for you, you'll just know it's right. You won't have to convince yourself or explain why. You'll just feel it.

Success may not happen right away, or as fast as you want, but if you love what you do, work hard, and have supportive family or friends, you can achieve your dreams.

Whether it's a money problem or a personal goal you want to reach, you need to set clear targets to aim for.

Working with family has pros and cons. It can be tough when you have to fight for what you think is fair.

You can't always wait for your boss to recognise your value. Whether it's a raise, equity, a promotion, or simply more creative freedom, if you don't ask for it, you won't receive it.

You don't need to be the smartest; just buy when people are selling and sell when people are buying.

When decisions are out of control and people fail you, rather than allowing it to discourage you, switch gears and drive yourself to pursue something new and extraordinary.

Embracing Change and Growth in Business

Change is constant. In all areas of life, we experience change. And in business, we want to see change in the form of growth. You want your business to excel, to expand, to be profitable and valuable. Sure, sometimes that can feel scary or unsettling, but good things often spring from discomfort.

At Z. Real Estate, I have worked hard to embrace changes within the business. I have seen a lot of change and an increase in value. And below I've outlined some of my learnings for you.

- Not everyone likes taking risks with money to try something new. People are often afraid of change, but without taking risks, you won't grow.
- Change can be good, even if it initially feels uncomfortable. It might not seem beneficial at first, but over time, you'll see its value.
- When it's time to try new things, trust yourself and believe it's the right decision for your career or business.
- In business, things don't always go as planned. You have to be flexible and adapt to make the best of the situation.
- Holding onto anger and resentment is toxic. It's always better to let go and focus on moving forward.
- You don't have to harm others to achieve your goals, especially when it involves family.
- Starting a business takes a lot of hard work – it's not all about the glamour. Success comes from dedication and effort.
- If you're passionate about something, give it your all. Dedication is key to making it successful.
- Even if you're the one in charge and have invested money, you still need to put in the effort and get your hands dirty.

Overcoming the Seven Major Barriers to Success

1. Jealousy

As my career skyrocketed, my income quadrupled, and my fame increased, the jealousy others had towards me also grew.

I think jealousy is the greatest human imperfection.

We all have it to some extent, but some people are consumed by it.

It eats at them; they see you soaring like a bird while they feel heavy like a stone. This person is dangerous because they are the anti-you. You are bright, happy, and aggressively pursuing your goals, while the jealous person is often unhappy, frustrated, and angered that you're achieving your dreams.

The difference between a jealous person and a naysayer is that the jealous person doesn't say no to your face, but instead to everyone else about you. They don't stop there – they'll try to create a revolt against you, spreading the 'truth' about you. Sadly, they probably believe it. Their goal is to expose the lies of your success to the world. Only then can they feel some peace. Jealousy is common. We all harbour a small jealous part of ourselves. After all, we are human. But by acknowledging this flaw, we can better ourselves. By identifying the little jealous spot within us, we can contain it and move on.

Try this exercise: A friend of yours, someone you like a lot, wins $10 million in the lottery. You see the post on Facebook or read about it in the newspaper. Your ego immediately reacts: *Why wasn't that me?* But you have a choice; you always have a choice. Recognise that's the jealous part of you speaking, not the whole you. Remind yourself that you want good things for the world, especially for those around you. Your friend is going to use that money for something great, and their success will eventually benefit you. If you support others' success, they will want to be a part of your life.

Surround yourself with successful people. Jealousy won't get you anywhere but alone. Letting go of it frees you to be the best version of yourself. You might have someone in your life who hopes you fail. If you don't yet, you probably will in the future. The more successful you become, the more likely it is. Don't strike back. Take the higher road. Keep doing your thing. People will hate, and that's okay. They're not hating you – they are projecting their own issues onto your success. Rise above. I've learnt to wish jealous people the best. And the real lesson is to stay humble and kind. Life is about change, and you won't be on top forever. Someone else will eventually take your place. Maybe it will be you! Don't fall prey to anyone else's jealousy. Success is the best revenge.

2. Stop Wanting Everything Done Yesterday: The Power of Patience

Success takes patience, and patience is something you can develop.

It's like planting seeds. You can water them, nurture them, and help them grow, but they still take time. You can't rush the process, no matter how hard you try. Success grows at its own pace. Just like a tree, we need to be patient with our own growth and progress. Sometimes, we need to focus on improving every part of our lives, just as the tree focuses on growing one branch at a time.

The key is to keep planting the right seeds and trusting the process, no matter how long it takes.

3. Let Go of Expectations: Finding Peace in Giving

One of the best ways to find peace in life is to stop expecting anything in return when you give to others. Giving – whether it's emotionally, financially, or mentally – shouldn't come with conditions. Too often, we expect people to reciprocate the way we would, but that only leads to disappointment. Not everyone shares your principles, values, or approach to life.

In both personal and professional relationships, don't expect something in return for your kindness. When you give without expectation, you free yourself from disappointment. Your goals and success are your own responsibility. You can't rely on others to get you there. Focus on your own path and count on yourself to achieve your dreams. Give freely, without expecting anything back, and watch how much peace and comfort it brings you.

4. Understanding Money: Why It's Not Everything

I wasn't born with money; I came from humble beginnings. Adversity is something everyone needs to experience to truly appreciate what money can do for you.

It would be easy for me to tell you not to worry about money, but I understand the struggle that comes with it. I've been there. Money isn't my driving force, but I can remember exactly when I realised I didn't want to go through life without it. Sure, money comes and goes. Some days, it's in my pocket, other days, it's out of my hands. You come into this world with nothing and you can't take it with you when you leave. We all face financial challenges at some point, and not everyone is going to be a millionaire. And that's okay.

As I've grown older, I've learned that true wealth comes from things that money can't buy: loved ones, values, beliefs, and spirituality. These are the things that really matter. I'm writing this chapter in Tulum, Mexico, at 35 years old. As I sit by the beach, sipping my morning coffee, watching the palm trees sway in the wind, I realise this is where true happiness lies for me. It's in the small moments, not in flashy events or expensive parties. Sure, I've been offered VIP access to exclusive events, but I've learned that true success isn't found in those places. It's in living simply and appreciating life for what it is.

Going to the gym, reading a good book, eating healthily, and enjoying a walk by the beach – those are the things that bring me joy. You don't need a lot of money to enjoy those experiences. They're priceless, and they're available to everyone. Material things, as tempting as they might be, shouldn't be at the top of your priority list. If they are, it might be time to reassess what really matters in your life. Money can make things easier, but it's not the source of true fulfilment. It's the small, everyday moments that truly enrich our lives.

5. Embracing Failure as Part of Success

One of my favourite movie scenes is from *Rocky Balboa* (2006), where he says, 'It's not about how hard you get hit, it's about how hard you can get hit and keep moving forward. That's how winning is done'.

Life is a journey, not a destination. Be patient, learn the skills, and focus on kindness – help others along your journey. There will always be problems in life, but if they aren't health-related, they are just solvable challenges. Don't overthink; become a problem solver.

Gratitude is one of the best ways to feel good about your situation. Never forget where you started and how far you've come. Be proud of your progress. There are people in hospitals fighting for their health, and people around the world without food or shelter. Be grateful for the now. Remember, there are always others in worse situations than you.

As Thomas Edison once said, 'I'm successful because I've had thousands of failures'. Failure is a necessary part of success. It's a step on the path to growth.

6. Building Unshakable Self-Belief

Not believing in yourself is one of the biggest barriers to success. If you can't trust your own abilities, it becomes difficult to take the necessary actions to move forward. Self-doubt will hold you back. The key to overcoming this is setting small, achievable goals that prove to yourself you are capable. These wins, no matter how small, will help you build your confidence.

Remember, success doesn't come overnight. It takes time and patience to build confidence. But each small success feeds your self-belief and propels you forward. You'll start noticing that what once seemed impossible becomes achievable. Eventually, you'll reach a point where self-doubt has no place in your life. You'll become unstoppable. Believe in yourself, even when others don't. Because if you don't believe in yourself, no one else will.

7. The Power of Persistence

One of my favourite movies is *The Founder*, which tells the story of how McDonald's became the global brand it is today. The movie highlights Ray Kroc, who started by selling milkshake machines door-to-door before discovering the McDonald's restaurant. At the end of the movie, he shares one key message with the world: persistence pays off. And I couldn't agree more.

I wouldn't be where I am today if I hadn't persisted. It was tempting to give up after three years of not making a dollar. It was hard, and I doubted myself at times because I'm human. But it was my persistence that kept me going and ultimately led to success.

Success rarely comes on the first try. The key is to keep going, keep trying, and never lose sight of your vision. You've got this – you're a born winner. Keep persisting.

Make Every Day Count: Mastering Mindset, Passion, and Performance

My philosophy is that when you love what you do, and it's something you're truly passionate about, you're always going to have the best day. It's all about your outlook, which applies to every aspect of life. Some of my favourite hobbies are playing cricket, making music, and training at the gym. One of the reasons I enjoy doing these things is that I'm truly happy.

If you can learn how to live in the moment, it will allow you to reset your attitude when something goes wrong. For example, if you receive a frustrating call at 9:00 am about the world falling apart, you're then prepared to compartmentalise the emotions attached to that specific situation and reboot your mentality for the rest of the day. You can only control what happens next, not what already transpired. Many people fall into the trap of living in the past and trying to rewrite history, which is impossible.

If you lose an account or a listing, what's done is done. There's usually nothing you can do about it, but what you can do is go get a new account or listing.

If you obsess over a missed goal or a lost listing, you won't be able to push forward and overcome those obstacles.

As Steve Jobs said, 'The people who are crazy enough to think they can change the world are the ones who do'.

Break the Mould: How I Built Attention in Real Estate

Throughout my career, I've discovered many fun and unique approaches to promoting both myself and Z. Real Estate I have also been very clear about the ways I did not want to promote myself or my business. I was the first original agent in Australia to create a rap to sell a multimillion dollar home, complete with dancers, Lamborghinis, Ferraris, and private jets. I didn't think twice about the image or what people would say about it. I rapped the ZOLD song with my team, and let me tell you, it reached millions of people! Other agents were incredulous, saying, 'Oh my gosh, look at what he's done again'. But my motive was singular: to grab attention and get people talking about us. As the saying goes in business, it's not about who you know; it's about who knows you.

The same bold approach applied when we first put a 'For Sale' sign in the area, replacing the usual 'Sold' with our ZOLD sticker. We received numerous calls from neighbours informing us that there was a spelling mistake on our board. We took the opportunity to educate them: 'You're not sold unless you're ZOLD'. Hearing those calls filled me with joy inside. Yes, it was working! Did I care what other agents thought? Not at all.

In business, self-belief is paramount. Never doubt yourself if you have an idea, and never let anyone tell you that you're not good enough or that it wouldn't work. While it's important to listen to advice, take it as inspiration to improvise, adapt, and ultimately do it better. Trust your instincts, follow what's in your heart, and go for it unapologetically. After all, breaking the mould often leads to the most remarkable success stories. Embrace your individuality, and remember that the most groundbreaking innovations come from those who dare to be different.

Leading with Purpose: Inspiring Teams to Perform at their Best

As a leader, your ability to inspire and motivate your team is crucial to the success of both your business and personal growth. The way you approach challenges, communicate with others, and foster a positive environment can have a profound impact on your team's performance and overall morale. This chapter focuses on the key elements of positive leadership, passion, and the mindset required to guide your team towards achieving their best. Whether you're a seasoned business owner or just starting out, adopting the principles of positive leadership will help you build a resilient, successful team that supports your vision.

Build Strong Client Relationships

Show genuine enthusiasm for helping clients find their dream home or make a smart investment. Get excited and help them feel excited too. Take away the pressure and ease their nerves – everyone gets nervous when making big decisions. No one has ever lost money in real estate in Australia, as long as you buy to hold. The more excited you are about the properties, the more excited they will be.

Always stay optimistic. You don't know what financial challenges your clients may be facing, or what's in their bank account. Take off your salesman hat and put yourself in their shoes. This builds trust, and positivity will inspire your clients to trust your expertise. When it's time to make a decision, they'll be ready to act, even in tough market conditions or with a tight budget.

Your passion for the industry doesn't end when the deal closes. Every time I meet a prospect I always add them on socials, comment on their posts so I'm continuously in front of them and their friends.

I continue to stay in touch with them, share market updates or tips on where to invest next.

Have a laugh and don't take your job so seriously. Enjoy every phone call and the process of every transaction. Send thank-you notes, check in occasionally, and be available for any future real estate needs. Happy clients will refer you to others.

Be Unapologetically You: The Power of Self-Belief and Authenticity

There's only one of you that looks like you out of eight billion people. How amazing is that? You are already special. Be that amazing, funny and incredible human that you are and bring out the best out in others around you. Life is full of challenges and there will always be people that will try to bring down your energy and doubt you but use it as fuel to get up and keep pushing forward.

Success is not something you pursue, it's something you attract. You can never tell a human being to change but you can inspire them by being a good example yourself. People will always question you and doubt you, but once you've made a decision that you want to work and you're willing to risk it all, stick to your gut feeling and make it all work. Don't doubt yourself for a second.

Human beings are judgmental, make sure when out in public, be careful of how you present yourself and act as you never know where or when your next deal will come from. You need to act professionally and be yourself at all times. Even if people talk about you, stay true to yourself.

Selling anything to anyone starts with a simple thing that you need to believe in yourself and the product you're representing, otherwise how do you expect others to believe you? You need to believe in who you are and not change for anyone.

As humans we are always evolving and changing from different stages of life. You are a different person in your 20s to who you are in your 30s. I've disconnected with friends who I hung around with from high school days. Your old friends may not support you, thinking they've known the person you were. Along this journey, though, you will come across people who share the same path and goals and will bring out your best as your mission, vision and values will be aligned with each other. Stay strong; the people you can trust will come through.

Always believe in yourself and others around you. When goals are shared between people there is a level of comfort and an aim to bring out the best in each other. Go out of your way to help others, never expect anything in return; you never know where your next deal will come from.

Everything in life happens for a reason and it happens for the best. People come into your life for a reason and it's meant to be. If you have been working with a tough client and it doesn't feel right, let it go, trust your gut and you can never be wrong.

You vs You: Compete Harder, Grow Stronger, Win Bigger

Sales in general is a very competitive industry; you're always pitching against your competition.

I believe you are your biggest competition. It's you versus you on a daily basis. I genuinely believe that there's no better salesman who's ever existed in the whole entire universe. This type of self-confidence is necessary.

The market is very competitive and there's only so much inventory in the luxury space, so when my competition sees me walking into a home after they've pitched there too, I know it's a war between me and other agents. Healthy competition is fair; if you can't look after your clients your competition will. I work hard so that my competitors can't keep up. What's great about the free market is that it helps you build a stronger business and become a tougher person. Every superhero needs a villain – someone who makes you work harder and get better every day.

Once you have reached your financial goal, it doesn't stop there. Money does not buy happiness; happiness is a choice. Don't get complacent and never forget where you've come from. Even when you feel like you've reached all your goals, there's always more you can do. Make your clients feel so valued that if they choose a competitor it will be the biggest regret of their life.

One person who inspires me is Sylvester Stallone. His story is inspirational; at 78 he's still looking strong and he's passionate about everything he does. If you chase the money, you will get burnt out but if you chase passion, you make a mark so make your passion your pay cheque.

I've always said, 'Let's open a door and see what's inside'. I don't focus on what I can't do because I believe that the possibilities are endless. I'm willing to make mistakes and learn from them. I don't get stuck in my situation, especially if it doesn't feel right. The day you stop learning is the day you get bored, and when you get bored, you lose your drive and excitement for what you're doing.

That said, it's important to understand that you can't say yes to every chance you get. There's a big difference between considering an opportunity and accepting it. You need to think about whether an opportunity is good for you, and sometimes, you must make those decisions quickly.

“

MONEY DOES NOT BUY HAPPINESS; HAPPINESS IS A CHOICE.

”

Usually, I trust my gut feeling, and that helps me make the right choices. Of course, my gut feeling is based on what I've learned and the lessons I've picked up over the years.

I also want to remind you that things won't always go the way you want. And that's okay. It's all about how you deal with those situations, how you keep pushing forward, and how you adjust.

My journey hasn't always been easy, and it has never been boring. Growing up poor as a refugee, my family and I faced many hard times. My parents couldn't find work, and while my dad did his best to provide enough food for us, we struggled. But we made it to Australia, a place full of opportunities. My life has been unpredictable, exciting, and sometimes very tough.

What we went through as kids is hard to explain unless you've lived it. This fight against poverty is where my strong motivation comes from – changing from having nothing to having almost everything. I am thankful to God for giving me the strength to make a positive impact on the world, and I have loved every moment of it.

The lessons and experiences I've gained from my many challenges are very valuable. The reason I'm writing this book is to share my story and insights to inspire others. Every successful person has faced problems; the bottom of the mountain is crowded because not many people want to climb to the top.

Greed Kills Deals: Understanding Value in a Real Market

One of the easiest ways to get into a negative mindset is by being greedy. I believe it's one of the worst traits a person can have, especially in business. This applies to anyone in any field, but I see it happen a lot with real estate developers and investors. I've probably sold more homes for developers and investors than anyone I know. When investors become greedy, it often leads to financial trouble.

For some reason, investors feel like they shouldn't lose money on the homes they build and invest in. Strangely, they understand that if they buy something, like Instagram stock at $100 and want to sell it at $70, they will lose money. Yet, if they spend $3 million on a house and its value drops to $2.5 million, they refuse to accept that loss. The reality is that market conditions determine the value of your investment, plain and simple.

Be a Leader, Not a Follower

Lions lead with courage; sheep follow the herd. The world needs more lions who stand out and make their own path!

The world wants to work with experts, not beginners.

You want to live a bigger and better life, and I WANT THIS FOR YOU TOO! Remember, you have the power to do this! YOU are in control NOW. At first, we all have control, but sometimes that control gets taken away and feels lost. The first step to living a bigger life is taking back that control, and it starts with knowing who you want to be. Think about the success you want to show the world – dream BIG. Does your life look like what you truly want?

Step 1: Get Over Yourself

- Every time you point one finger at someone, there are three fingers pointing at yourself.
- Don't talk behind others, you will be left behind.
- Giving starts the process of receiving in life. Become a good giver and not a taker. If you don't recommend something to yourself, don't recommend it to others.

Step 2: Take Control

- You are where you are in your life because of you and hard work. If you're not happy, take control and change it.
- Don't leave things up to luck. Luck is when preparation meets an opportunity. You're in charge of your future but take baby steps. Start small and then go big. If it's meant to be it will be.

Step 3: Persuade Others

- People want what they can't have. Take it away, it makes them want it more.
- Don't tell people what they want to hear, tell them what they need to hear.
- People sometimes need time to think: don't be a pushy salesman, be an adviser you will get more respect.

- Become a problem-solver: Offer a solution. Don't add more stress and anxiety to what they already have. Focus on the solution not the problem.
- Build rapport and don't give them too many options as you will get them confused. Offering too many options will get them confused, give them one or two options to pick from.

Embrace Your Power: Rise Above Negativity

In the end, it's important to realise that you can't always change other people, and you're going to encounter some difficult individuals on your path to success. Instead of trying to combat their bad attitudes, focus on your level of likeability, earn lots of money, and WIN at life. Stay committed to operating on a higher level. That's the energy you need, and it will make you a force in getting everything you want. That's why you're reading this right now, isn't it? To learn how to get more of what you want?

Earn Your Freedom: The Power of Money and Hard Work

Money might not be everything, but it plays a major role in your life. Being alive can be expensive. At its most basic level, money represents survival and freedom, but you don't want to live a basic life. You work hard and crave a great life with all the accoutrements that come along with it. For you, more money means the freedom to live your life however you want.

Financial freedom is a choice: put your head down and get to work – work until you have no energy left and have given it your best.

Creating Your Own Luck through Preparation and Action

In real estate, luck isn't just about chance – it's when preparation meets opportunity. I embody this principle. I don't just wait for the phone to ring; I'm a hustler who goes out and creates opportunities. I know that the money lies with people, and I actively nurture those relationships. By asking the right questions and engaging with my network, I'm not just hoping for luck to come my way, I'm making it happen. So I'll keep chasing those opportunities, and I'll continue to build my luck in the real estate world!

They're not 'lucky'. They just took action. They just chose not to be afraid. They worked through the discomfort until it felt okay.

Everyone has the ability. If anyone has done it, then you can too. You can be 'one of them'– it's just a change in how you think.

"

LUCK IS WHAT HAPPENS WHEN
PREPARATION MEETS OPPORTUNITY.

"

Change Yourself

You cannot have more than what you have now until you change the way you act.

Everybody hopes that things will get better, but the future doesn't improve with just hope – it improves with plans. As the American entrepreneur Jim Rohn would say, 'If you wish to be successful, study success. If you wish to be happy, study happiness. If you wish to be wealthy, study wealth'. Do not leave things to chance – make them a study. Some people go through the day with their fingers crossed. How can it ever be enough? You must study what can change your social, spiritual, and personal life.

Change What You Don't Like

If you dislike how things are with you, if they are not enough, if they do not suit you and definitely do not please you – **CHANGE THEM.** I say you should work to change your life because I know that you can! You can transform yourself today by making the right choice.

I was born in poverty in the war zone of Afghanistan and don't have many good memories of my childhood. My family had to escape from there. We migrated to a country where we were not welcomed, 14 people sustained by living in a two-bedroom apartment.

What I hate the most about the Middle Eastern and even some European countries is the class divide. You are either very rich or very poor, and the poor are never heard or paid any heed to. That is where my drive and hunger came from. Achieving financial freedom and changing things for the greater good became my purpose in life. I wish to give to the community without expecting anything in return. I wish to educate those in need, bring out the best in all, and make everyone feel special and good about themselves.

The hardest part of my career wasn't starting a brand or business. The hardest part was deciding to believe that I could do it – **anyone can**. Life wasn't designed to give us what we want, but those who believe in themselves get what they deserve.

Self-Confidence

Where does self-confidence come from? It comes from knowing that you've done your best and achieved the desired results. If you hold a meeting or make a phone call, make sure that the meeting or call gets the finest of you. When you finally seal the deal with a client after numerous unsuccessful attempts, your self-confidence is bound to grow.

Looking good, feeling good, and making others feel good about themselves all boost your self-confidence. You need to step out of your comfort zone and keep on learning to grow. The more you learn, the more you earn, and the more confidence you gain.

Self-Belief

I failed three years in a row in my career and had no money for anything I liked. Everyone told me to quit, including my family members, but I persisted. All that I am today is the result of my **self-belief**.

There might come times when you feel that your friends are laughing at you, your goals, and your dreams. It is then that you should remind yourself not to seek anyone else's approval. People's opinions do not pay your bills. Their opinion is not your reality.

Be consistent. Your hard work will always pay off, and remember that one day things will turn around.

Self-Reliance

Look up to yourself. Not everyone does what they are supposed to do, so don't expect anything from others, and they will not have the power to let you down. Always rely on yourself, hold yourself responsible, learn from your mistakes, and don't stop until the goal is reached.

Self-Discipline

Have the ability to get rid of distractions. Do not waste time on one-hour coffee breaks, and have the self-control to say no to a cheeseburger.

Tell yourself, 'I will do the best job I can!' There will be mistakes, but hey, we are human. You must ultimately have the self-discipline to know that if you want to live extraordinarily, you must be extraordinary. The contentment of giving your all and earning your reward will be the most satisfying experience.

FIVE WAYS TO HELP OTHERS BELIEVE IN THEMSELVES

1. Encourage them
2. Acknowledge the good
3. Challenge them
4. Listen to them
5. Recognise good decision-making

THE POWER OF VALUE

The late Jim Rohn said it best: 'We get paid for bringing value to the marketplace. It takes time to bring value to the marketplace, but we get paid for the value, not the time.'

This statement encapsulates the essence of success in business and life. You are not paid for how long you work, but for the value you bring to the world. The marketplace doesn't care about your time. It cares about the impact you make, the solutions you provide, and how you serve others.

The reality of the marketplace is that we pay for value, not time. If someone is only paid $17 per hour, it's because they are not bringing enough value to justify a higher rate. They might be a valuable friend, sibling, or community member, but to the marketplace, they have not yet demonstrated their worth.

This is the economic reality we all face. If you want to earn more, you must become more valuable. It's not the job that makes you the money, it's the skill. It's not about waiting for a raise – it's about increasing your worth and becoming irreplaceable.

You can't demand more money. It's not about waiting for someone to hand you a raise. It's about becoming more valuable to the marketplace.

Think about it: Why would someone pay you $100 per hour? Because you've shown your value. You bring something unique, you solve problems, and you make life easier for others. You've invested in yourself, and it shows in your skills, expertise, and the way you engage with the world.

Becoming more valuable is not only possible, it's essential. The marketplace rewards value, and it's a continuous cycle of growth and improvement.

Here's the secret: Work harder on yourself than you do on your job.

To become valuable in the marketplace, invest in your own growth. Ask yourself: How many books have you read in the last year? How many seminars have you attended? Are you constantly working on developing new skills and improving your mindset?

Your value is directly related to your personal growth and the knowledge you acquire. The more you grow, the more valuable you become.

Results are the ultimate teacher. Your results will show you where you are succeeding and where you need to improve. The more phone calls you make, the better you will get. The more action you take, the more lessons you will learn.

In sales, it's not about making a certain number of calls – it's about your attitude towards those calls. Do you view them as opportunities, or as obstacles? Your mindset will determine your success.

If you find yourself struggling, sometimes the best affirmation is the most honest one: *I am broke.*

Put it on your refrigerator or somewhere you'll see it every day. Let it serve as a reminder that you can change your situation. It might not be pleasant to admit, but acknowledging where you are is the first step towards changing it. When you face the truth, you can take responsibility for it, and that's where real change begins.

The key to increasing your value in the marketplace is simple: invest in yourself, develop your skills, and become someone who solves problems, adds value, and takes action. Your worth is not determined by the hours you work, but by the impact you make. Keep learning, keep growing, and let your results speak for themselves. The more valuable you become, the more opportunities you'll create, and the more success you'll attract.

GOAL SETTING

Write and Set a Time Frame

Once a goal is written down, but lacks a time frame, it becomes meaningless. You need to set daily, weekly, monthly, quarterly, and annual goals. Each goal should have a deadline, making it concrete and achievable.

For example, when I invest money in real estate I don't wait for the market to go up, I work within the existing market and I buy very well. The money in real estate lies in buying well when you have done your homework. Once you've invested your money you need an exit strategy; if you invest one million dollars on a property, you need to flip it, develop it, or even a simple interior and styling change could make at least $50,000. The smartest people are those who use somebody else's money: the bank.

So when you invest, set your goal, be specific and make sure you put a timeline on it.

Tell Someone Important

After setting your goals, share them with someone important to you. This creates an added incentive to accomplish them. Goals that are kept secret lack commitment. Just as we celebrate marriage publicly, pick someone you trust and share your goals with them to give them more weight.

High and Low Goals

Set both high and low goals. High goals are your aspirations; low goals are the minimum requirements to keep your job. Make sure you are clear on the minimum expectations for your job by asking your supervisor or HR department. Your low goals should also cover your living expenses, so you're always secure.

Activity and Results

You should set both activity and results-driven goals.

- **Result goals** are straightforward and self-explanatory.
- **Activity goals** focus on the actions that lead to results, such as new presentations, follow-up meetings, and calls to prospects. These should be broken down into weekly, monthly, quarterly, and annual goals.

Small Time Frames

It's easier to focus on activity results in smaller time frames rather than long periods. Break down your year into 12 monthly segments, and further break each month into weekly goal periods for better focus and concentration.

Don't Stack

If you don't reach your goals in one period, don't stack them. Similarly, if you exceed your goals in one period, don't reduce your goals for the next period. Your goals are meant to keep you focused, so don't change them based on short-term results. Stacking goals defeats their purpose.

Track Your Goals Versus Your Results

Track your goals versus results and activities. By filling out reports daily or weekly, you can stay on top of your progress. All professionals track their performance, and sales professionals are no different. You cannot score without keeping score. Weekly reporting of activities and results is crucial for tracking success.

No Excuses

Once your goals are set, don't allow yourself to make excuses. Life will always present challenges – whether it's illness, family issues, bad weather, or car problems. The world doesn't care about the storms you face; they only want to know if you brought in the ship.

Adopt the habit of saying NEAT: **No Excuses Accepted Today**. There are two kinds of people: those who find a way, and those who find excuses. Be the kind of person who goes over, under, around, or through any obstacle in your path.

By implementing these goal-setting practices, you'll maintain clarity, direction, and drive towards achieving the success you desire. Keep your goals focused, tracked, and, most importantly, action-driven.

"

**ONCE YOUR GOALS ARE SET,
DON'T ALLOW YOURSELF TO MAKE EXCUSES.**

"

BUILDING CONNECTIONS

FIRST IMPRESSIONS

There's a well-known, unattributed proverb that states, 'A first impression is always the last impression'.

People will remember the way you appear when you first meet them, so it's important to look and act your best when meeting someone for the first time. The first impression is made in less than five seconds and is the most powerful influencer on how people respond to you.

In sales, the open starts with the impression you make. You get judged on your body language, energy, outfit, and most importantly, how you shake a client's hand. Make it a point to come in with style, confidence, and deliver your message with enthusiasm and control. It will set the tone for the whole deal. The energy you put out is the energy you will receive. I create wealth for the rich, so I like to act like the rich – be it in my suit, watch, or car.

In fact, I was the first 25 year old driving a Lamborghini in an area where the average house price was $400,000. When I drove up to their driveway, I was told not to show up in a Lamborghini as clients would think I sold drugs, rather than believing that I really was successful at my job. But with every deal I closed, people came closer to the realisation of who I really am. I will never forget where I have come from, but sometimes people do forget who they are when they put money first. In life, people will judge you anyway, so just let them do it.

I invested in a car when everyone told me not to. They thought it was silly to spend that much on a car, but I used it as a prospecting tool. I would park it anywhere and take every kid for a ride if they asked for it. Eventually, I made sure that each kid walked away with my business card in hand so they could pass it to their parents.

I wasn't offered such chances as a kid, so my goal is to make someone's day better and give them the vision that anything in life is possible if you put your heart and mind to it. We live in a materialistic world; you and I might not be, but it is a reality.

Money talks, it shows, and the fact remains that we are doing this to make more money. The Lamborghini elevated my status to the level that I envisioned because I believed it to achieve it.

It doesn't take money to make money; it takes courage.

Three Ways to Create a Positive First Impression

1. **Be on Time.** If you're meeting a client for the first time, they will not be interested in your excuses for running late. I advise my staff to show up 10 minutes early to any appointment. The old saying goes, 'If you're on time, you're late'. If you're ten minutes early, you're on time; if you're late, well, it's unacceptable. Arriving early is much better than arriving late, and it's the first step towards creating a great impression. You only get one chance to make a good first impression, so make sure to leave a good one.
2. **Be You, Be Yourself.** The best way to create a good first impression is to be real, be yourself, your true, authentic self. This is your biggest advantage in life. I love it when people ask me, 'What's my point of difference?' There are over seven billion people in the world, and there is only one person who's me. I am original – you can never pretend to be someone you're not. By owning your real self, you feel more confident, build trust, and earn the respect and integrity from your daily clients.
3. **Compliment with Positive Statements.** Before I meet with a client, I always make sure I've put on good aftershave. Not

> only do you have to look good, but you need to smell good too. I often don't give too many compliments to potential prospects. Keep it at one or two maximum compliments; that's more than enough. Too much flattery will lead to suspicion. I've trained hundreds of salespeople, and I get shocked by how they compliment their prospects. Their compliments are very basic and often unrelated to the conversation, such as 'Nice suit', 'Nice watch', 'Nice office', or 'Nice home'. Personal compliments like these should be reserved for your friends and family.

The instinct to be both genuine and accessible is something that comes naturally to me. I've always been a people person – someone who shakes everyone's hands and looks everyone in the eyes. I also believe these are attributes that can be taught and learned if you set your mind to them and really put yourself out there.

Too often, when people are engaged in conversation with someone, they're scanning the room for someone more important. I see this behaviour all the time, specifically among salespeople, and even more specifically within the real estate trade. It may be a natural impulse, but it's still wrong. What's worse is when someone treats people in the service industry as if they're beneath them.

Trust me when I tell you that when you only focus your attention and efforts on those you feel can deliver you value or make you money, it will not go unnoticed. The old saying, 'Don't judge a book by its cover' is absolutely true. Just because someone isn't wearing fancy clothing or driving an expensive car doesn't mean they're insignificant. You never know who you're going to meet in any given circumstance, and making incorrect assumptions based on outward appearance is a major mistake.

Today, more than ever, there are extremely successful people who dress casually – they don't necessarily opt for suits and ties anymore, like they did when they were first starting out. It used to be that, based on someone's outfit, you could discern whether they were a labourer or a professional, but that's no longer the case. In our current society, you could be talking to a billionaire who looks like he's homeless.

As a salesperson, it's critical to make everyone feel like a VIP. When you do this, the same level of respect will be granted in return, and it will help you in the long run. Of course, you can't do it for that reason; it's just the universe's way of maintaining balance. It's the same concept as being philanthropic.

When you assume a social responsibility to give back to those less fortunate, that sends good karma in your direction. If you stop giving, you stop receiving. Giving starts the process of receiving.

Case in point: I once made a sale because the doorman at my apartment building in South Yarra introduced me to a buyer out of the goodness of his heart. And do you know what I did? I gave that doorman a $2000 referral cheque. He wasn't expecting it, and he didn't make the introduction for that reason, but because of his generosity, he benefited. Further, he would never have known I was a real estate agent if I hadn't talked to him and got to know him. That's just who I am, and it's been an enormous advantage to me throughout my career.

I find people interesting, and I treat everyone with the utmost respect, no matter who they are or how much money they have. I want to hear their stories and ask them questions. Just recently, my friend and I went to a concert, and we purchased general admission tickets because the VIP section was sold out. Typically, I'd be in the VIP section, hanging out with event organisers, owners of multimillion dollar corporations, and other business magnates. But instead of mingling with those people, I met a wide variety of thriving professionals – a doctor, a private equity guy, and a personal trainer. They were all equally as interesting to me as someone with a boldfaced name. And the possibility that one of them will eventually connect me with someone else who has an impact on my life is very feasible.

The point is, getting to know people – no matter who they are or who you think they are – is the best way to expand your personal and professional networks. And you should never stifle that impulse.

> **"**
>
> **AS A SALESPERSON, IT'S CRITICAL TO MAKE EVERYONE FEEL LIKE A VIP.**
>
> **"**

CONNECTING THROUGH KINDNESS – THE POWER OF GENUINE RELATIONSHIPS

In every interaction, there's one thing that can make all the difference: kindness. Whether you're dealing with a colleague, a teammate, or a loved one, the ability to make someone feel valued is an invaluable skill. True success comes not just from achieving your own goals, but from nurturing relationships built on respect, empathy, and genuine care for others.

To be both successful and caring, take the time to be genuinely interested in those around you. People thrive when they feel recognised, so offer your encouragement and let them know they matter. A simple 'well done' or 'I appreciate you' can go a long way in building strong, supportive relationships.

Celebrating successes is vital, but so is forgiving mistakes. No one is perfect, and the ability to acknowledge and learn from mistakes – both your own and others' – fosters growth and trust. Saying 'sorry' when needed and accepting apologies graciously can strengthen bonds and build mutual respect. Criticise only when necessary, and always in a constructive way. It's not about pointing out flaws; it's about offering guidance and support for improvement.

The most powerful form of kindness is listening. To listen well is to show that you value the other person's thoughts, ideas, and feelings. Learning from others, showing empathy, and offering love and support will enrich both your relationships and your life.

And don't forget the joy of sharing happiness. When you spread joy to those around you, it creates a ripple effect. Happiness grows when it's shared, and when you make others happy, that positivity often comes back to you. In turn, it strengthens your relationships, builds lasting friendships, and fosters a culture of collaboration.

Remember this: sharing happiness never runs out of fashion. Be kind to others, and kindness will find its way back to you. This cycle of goodwill creates deeper connections, fuels teamwork, and inspires those around you to do the same.

THE IMPORTANCE OF CLIENT RELATIONSHIPS IN SALES

Relationships with clients are everything in the sales industry. Even when nothing is happening, it's important to remain in close contact and check in periodically.

This is especially relevant in today's market, where interest rates are sitting at 6.5 percent, and people are scared to invest.

We have to remind them that it's easy to make money in a hot market. Everyone else does the same but in order to make money you have to take a risk; some of the best businesses have been developed during the toughest times.

Educate clients on investing. Remind them when they invest, they should be thinking about long-term goals, not short term. If you have an unrealistic vendor who wants more than the market value, be honest with them. Never make a promise on a price just to get the listing or to tell the vendor what they want to hear. This approach loses credibility and clients. Be honest and straightforward from the beginning and educate clients on the marketplace. It's a small industry where people talk to friends and family.

Agents often try to avoid confrontation. Often, when there is no movement on a property, some may avoid calling their clients. Instead, make contact to explain that you're working diligently. Check in every week; they will appreciate you rather than blame you.

When agents avoid clients, there's a good chance they'll be irritated when you finally check in. By staying in touch, your clients know you're paying attention, and they feel like you're in it together. This gives them hope that you can still save the deal, and ultimately, they'll likely let you extend their listing when it expires. And that's the goal.

HOW TO NETWORK

The more people you meet, the more opportunities you create in order to sell more, your network is your net worth.

Here are some strategies to help you network effectively:

- **Networking is Time Management.** Networking is essentially a time management function. The better you manage your time, the more people you'll be able to meet and, ultimately, sell to. Continuously ask yourself, 'What's the best use of my time right now?' 80 percent of your results will come from 20 percent of your activities. Identify the 20 percent of activities that have the biggest impact and dedicate your time to mastering them.
- **Manage Your Prospect List.** Always keep an updated prospect list with you. The list should include the company name, contact name, phone number, and email if possible. This list should be stored both digitally (on your laptop) and physically (on paper). Aim to maintain a minimum of 100 names at all times. This ensures you always have people to call and engage with.
- **Develop Your Prospect List Consistently.** Managing your prospect list is an ongoing task. This can be done before or after the traditional workday. Consistent management of your list ensures you're always building your network.
- **Look for New Prospects.** Schedule regular time to prospect. Each week, set aside a specific time on your calendar for prospecting, as you would for any important appointment. Whether you use an electronic or paper calendar, make this time non-negotiable. Treat it with the same level of importance as meetings or client appointments.

- **Commit to Prospecting Every Day.** Make prospecting a daily habit. Aim to spend at least two hours each day on this activity. The more consistent you are, the more results you'll see in the long run. During your prospecting time, don't let yourself get distracted unless it's something urgent.
- **Get Comfortable with Discomfort.** To accomplish your goals, you must push yourself out of your comfort zone every day. If you feel comfortable tomorrow, you'll instantly recognise that you haven't challenged yourself enough. Growth happens outside of comfort.
- **Overcome Objections and Rejections.** We all face objections and rejections, but you can either find a solution or make excuses. Common excuses include, 'It's too early to call', 'It's Monday, they're busy', or 'It's after 5:00 pm'. Recognise these mental tricks and break free from them. Make a list of your excuses and remind yourself: '**No Excuses Accepted Today**'.
- **Control Your Calendar.** Once a prospect agrees to meet you, make sure to schedule it in your calendar immediately. Either send them a calendar invite or have your assistant do so. The better you control your calendar, the better you can manage your time, and the more productive you will be.

By following these networking tips, you can maximise your time, overcome objections, and continuously expand your network, ultimately leading to greater sales success.

Building Impactful Connections in a Modern World

When I first got into real estate social media wasn't that big. Business cards were the way to build connections. Now we have social media where everything is available on your fingertips; you can literally get in contact with anyone all over the world and connect with them via socials. All you have to do is reach out to them and ask for a connection.

Here's another secret: When I want someone's business, I email, text, or add them on social media immediately after the meeting. Often, I'll grab their business card, shake their hand, say goodbye, then turn the corner where they can't see me, stop, and send them a direct message via socials or write an email. The key is to correspond before they've checked their phone or computer.

Wow, they think, *This guy is good.*

In the digital age, all it takes is a right-click on someone's email signature, and boom – you've saved their information forever. Everyone is available on all platforms so to me business cards are more of a 90s theme. As time changes you need to keep up with technology and adapt.

Building Recognition and Connecting with Your Network

Getting people to know your name is one of the most powerful steps towards growing your personal brand or business. But how do you make an impression that sticks? It starts with building strong relationships and getting yourself out there.

1. **Be Friendly and Leverage Your Network**
   Start with the people you already know. Use the contacts in your smartphone to create a list of all the fabulous people in your life. Start by calling your high school friends, family members and ask them to spread the word. Your family and loved ones will support you more than anyone else, whether you're selling clothes, coffee, or real estate. These people are the ones you'll first introduce to your products, services, and events. Keep them updated with clever announcements or by inviting them to an open home. Early in my career, I made a habit of attending networking events or seminars. I would show up wherever there were people, and it always resulted in client referrals, new leads, and cash in my pocket. These connections became my word-of-mouth advocates and social media promoters. They will introduce you and put you in front of the right people. Everyone knows one or two people in the industry that you are in.
2. **Be Passionate and Infectious**
   Enthusiasm is contagious. If you bring the energy, people will want to work with you, regardless of whether you're new to the game or a senior consultant. Passion creates opportunities and invites collaboration.
3. **Act Now – Procrastination Is Your Enemy**
   There's no time like the present. If you hesitate, the opportunity may disappear. Seize it when it presents itself, because it may not come knocking twice. Procrastination sends a message that you lack enthusiasm and initiative,

and it can sap your confidence. Start your day with a plan, stay productive, and use your downtime wisely, whether it's hitting the gym, engaging in relaxing activities, or planning for the future.

4. **Balance Is Overrated – Commit Fully**
   Give your full energy to whatever you're doing. Work hard while you're working, and play hard when you're off the clock. People are drawn to your dedication and enthusiasm. Time management is essential. Organise your day to accommodate disruptions so your priorities stay intact. When you're with family, enjoy them, when you're at work focus on doing just that and when you go home learn to switch off. I know it's easier said than done. Real estate is unpredictable.
5. **Master Your To-Do List**
   Do you have a to-do list? If not, start one immediately. At the end of each day, reflect on what you've accomplished and set bigger goals for the next day. Success comes from knowing what truly matters and prioritising it. Once these are in place, tackle your most challenging tasks first. Once that's conquered, move on to the next items on your agenda. There's nothing more satisfying than crossing off tasks from your list. As Ingvar Kamprad, the founder of IKEA, once said, 'The most dangerous poison is the feeling of achievement. The antidote is to think every evening about what can be done better tomorrow'.

Winning People Over with Authentic Connections

Everyone is born with varying degrees of natural charisma, but charm is a skill that can be learned and refined through practice. Since many people on social media have asked me how to attract others and get them to like you, let's dive into **Zed's Charm Talk**!

Charm, my friends, is the art of having an appealing personality. While I know some successful but rude people, I believe their success is often temporary or empty – because they're ultimately unhappy. We're more likely to build strong personal and professional relationships with people we like – those who are agreeable, kind, and funny. In short, charming people get their way.

You already know this. So why are there so few funny and happy people out there? It's because our entire lives, we've been told to tone it down. I'm here to tell you to **tone it up**!

How I Charm People on the Phone

Customer service representatives often deal with rude customers. Being nice automatically makes you stand out and increases the likelihood of getting what you want. Plus, it feels better. Why have an unpleasant encounter when you can create a positive one?

How I Charm People in Cafes and Restaurants

I always take the time to be nice to cafe staff and restaurant managers. Instead of barking out my coffee order, I ask, 'What's your name?' or 'How's your day going?' Most people don't ask. Most people don't care. But we *should.*

It only takes a minute to make an investment in others, and in return, they're more likely to make an investment in us. Whether it's putting a little extra care into my coffee or sharing a genuine smile, these small gestures perpetuate a charmed day.

The Value of Being Nice to Everyone

When I first got into real estate, I was told to view everyone as an opportunity – and to always be nice. To this day, whenever someone walks past me, I might say, 'I love your dog! What type is it? What's her name? She's adorable!' Or I'll compliment their outfit or tell them their baby is so cute.

"

IT ONLY TAKES A MINUTE TO MAKE
AN INVESTMENT IN OTHERS.

"

I've found that people appreciate this. A sincere compliment rewards both the receiver and the giver – and it's free! Try it. Smile while doing it, and you'll double the effect. A brief, uplifting encounter will boost your mood because you've lifted someone else's.

Charm is about creating connections, building trust, and spreading positivity. And when you master the art of charm, you'll find that people are naturally drawn to you – both personally and professionally.

How I Build Trust with My Real Estate Clients

Building trust with my clients is the foundation of my real estate business, and over the years, I've learned that the key to success lies in being authentic, dependable, and supportive. When I first started in real estate, I quickly realised that success wasn't just about closing deals or showing properties – it was about building trust, understanding, and connection with the people I work with. From the very first conversation, I make it my mission to create relationships that go beyond just the transaction. In this business, trust is everything. My clients don't want to feel like they're just another sale or deal; they want to know that I'm looking out for their best interests and that I'm here to guide them through the entire process with honesty and care.

I take the time to understand their needs, concerns, and dreams. I work tirelessly to help them make the best decisions, even if it means steering them away from a house they may have fallen in love with but might not be the right fit. This level of support is what fosters trust, leading to long-term relationships and repeat business. For me, it's never just about Zelling a house; it's about being a trusted adviser, a friend, and someone who's always there for them – whether they're buying their first home, their forever home, or looking to sell years down the road.

This mindset has become the cornerstone of my work, and it's what truly sets me apart in a competitive industry. Here's how I approach it:

- **Honesty and Transparency.** Being straightforward is essential in building trust. If I see a problem with a property or the market conditions aren't favourable, I don't hide it. For example, when I showed a client a house with an outdated kitchen, I didn't sugarcoat it. I said, 'This kitchen might need work, but it has great potential if you're willing to remodel'. They appreciated my openness, which strengthened our connection.

- **Active Listening and Personalization.** I make it a point to understand what my clients truly need. One client mentioned that they didn't want a large yard because of their busy lifestyle. Instead of showing them every house on the market, I focused on low-maintenance properties. This saved them time and frustration and showed that I'm genuinely focused on what works best for them.
- **Quick and Reliable Communication.** I know how important it is to be responsive. Whether it's late at night or over the weekend, I prioritise responding to messages quickly. One client, who was anxious about finding the right home, mentioned how much they appreciated my prompt replies. It helped them feel more confident and assured in their decision-making.
- **Delivering on Promises.** Following through on commitments is a must in real estate. For example, I once promised a client I would send them a home inspection report the next day, and I did, even though my schedule was packed. These small but meaningful actions show that they can rely on me to keep my word.
- **Offering Value Beyond the Sale.** I see my clients as more than just transactions. I genuinely want to help them in all aspects of their journey. Recently, I gave a client advice on

boosting their home's kerb appeal before listing it. They were thankful for my insights, and it helped them feel supported even when we weren't actively buying or selling.

- **Patience and Understanding.** Real estate can be a stressful process, and sometimes it takes time to find the right fit. I worked with one couple who had trouble finding the right home for months, and they were feeling discouraged. I kept a calm approach and reassured them that the right property would appear. Eventually, we found the perfect home, and they appreciated my patience throughout the process.
- **Protecting Their Best Interests.** My goal is to ensure my clients make the right choice, not just to close a deal. If I see a home that has good features but serious flaws – like poor location or layout – I'll be upfront about it. Sometimes, I might even say, 'This isn't the right home for you'. I do this because I want my clients to know I'm looking out for their long-term satisfaction, not just pushing a sale.
- **Maintaining High Standards.** I won't show my clients properties that don't meet my standards. Everyone has a different idea of what makes a house a good fit, but I only present homes I believe are worth considering. I guide my clients to the right property at their pace. When I steer them away from a bad choice, they gain confidence in my ability to lead them towards the perfect one.

By focusing on these key principles – honesty, active listening, clear communication, following through, providing value beyond the sale, showing patience, and always prioritising their best interests – I've been able to build long-lasting relationships with my clients. They know they can trust me, and that trust has turned into repeat business and many happy homeowners.

The Power of Personal Connections in Sales

To be a successful salesperson, building strong relationships with your clients is essential. To achieve this, you need to pay attention to who your clients are and understand their goals. Take the time to ask about their loved ones, pets, and any special occasions in their lives. Even recalling a specific memory that brings them joy can go a long way. But most importantly, remembering their names is crucial. It shows you value them and are genuinely invested in getting to know them.

In my case, I built my entire business around open houses. Some agents cold call door-to-door, while others 'farm' neighbourhoods by sending letters to every mailbox. Others rely on their sphere of influence, especially if they're well-connected. My approach to building my career and client base was to attend open houses as frequently as possible. This helped me learn about available inventory while also building my network.

At these open houses, I treated each interaction like a game – gathering as much information as possible about attendees and committing it to memory. I started with their names. My motivation for this method stemmed from my experiences attending other agents' open houses, where I was shocked by the poor service. Agents would often be reading a book or watching sports on their phones, dressed inappropriately, or even giving off unpleasant vibes. I'd walk into these open houses only to be barely acknowledged, asked to 'please register your name at the door', and left to explore the house alone without any assistance from the agent.

This experience inspired me to take a completely different approach. When hosting an open house, I would arrive early with a prominent sign to advertise. In the early days of my career, I ensured that my open house signs were placed at key intersections by 8:00 am, with my photo on them to promote my brand to as many locals as possible. I made sure I was well-dressed and full of energy. Typically, 20 to 30 people would visit, and my goal was to establish a personal connection with every client within the first 30 seconds of meeting them.

I would greet each person with, 'Welcome, I'm Zed. What's your name? … John Smith, great! And your kids? Fred, Michael, and Samantha? Excellent, it's nice to meet you all. What are you looking for?' With just three simple questions, I started to build that connection. After that, I let them explore the house, but continued to engage them.

As each new visitor arrived, I asked the same three questions, continuing to build personal connections. For example, I might approach John Smith and his family again by asking, 'John, how did you like that kitchen? Isn't it fabulous? Please let me know if there's anything I can do for you. Fred, Michael, and Angel, are you enjoying yourselves? Would you like to check out the backyard and play on the swing set?' This was not about closing the deal immediately but about fostering a human connection.

Once the children came back inside, I would ask about their experience on the swing set, while continuing the conversation with the parents. If they weren't satisfied with the house, I would inquire about what features they felt were missing and take note of their specific needs. Understanding their dislikes helped me find better-suited alternatives. The key was in creating personal situations that encouraged clients to share more about their preferences.

I often compare real estate to matchmaking. The more inventory and client knowledge you have, the quicker you can make the perfect match. Sometimes it requires viewing multiple homes to find the right fit, but once the client sees your expertise, they will trust you to find them the perfect property – whether it's listed or off-market.

This approach isn't exclusive to real estate. It applies to any field where building relationships is key – whether in hospitality, banking, law, or medicine. Knowledge is power. Researching clients online through platforms like Facebook and Instagram can give you insights into their preferences, allowing you to offer a more tailored experience.

> **"ULTIMATELY, BUILDING EMOTIONAL CONNECTIONS AND FOSTERING COMFORT AND TRUST ARE THE CORNERSTONES OF A SUCCESSFUL BUSINESS RELATIONSHIP."**

For instance, when staying at a luxury hotel, I am always impressed when the staff anticipates my preferences – like having my favourite drink waiting in my room. Similarly, mortgage brokers who understand their clients' needs can offer valuable advice on refinancing or reinvestment opportunities.

While not every initial interaction will lead to a sale, being prepared for future encounters is vital. I remember most client details mentally and also take notes on their sign-in sheets. For example, John Smith lives on Beach Road, has three kids (Fred, Michael, and Angel), and is looking for a six-bedroom house with a gourmet kitchen.

By addressing clients by name and referencing their preferences in future conversations, you show that you are attentive and genuinely care about their needs. This will leave a lasting impression. Understanding and prioritising your clients' needs is essential, not just in sales, but in any profession. Just as a professional athlete prepares for their game, you must approach each open house with the same level of focus and preparation.

Being aware of the room and your surroundings, and understanding the people you interact with, is critical to creating successful and meaningful connections. Ultimately, building emotional connections, encouraging clients to share personal information, and fostering comfort and trust are the cornerstones of a successful business relationship.

The Power of Listening: How Understanding Clients Leads to Better Results

One of the most important lessons I've learned in my career is the power of listening. It's easy to think that being a great salesperson means talking non-stop and showing off how much you know. Early on, I used to make that mistake. I would jump into conversations with clients, eager to explain every detail, thinking that the more I said, the better I could serve them. But over time, I realised that the opposite is often true.

What I've come to understand is that the best way to show my expertise isn't by dominating the conversation – it's by really listening. When a client talks to me, I make sure I'm fully present. I let them express what they need, what they're looking for, and what's important to them. After they've said what's on their mind, I'll respond with a simple comment to show I've truly understood. I've found that this approach builds trust and helps me connect with them in a more meaningful way.

Listening first gives me the chance to tailor my response to what the client really wants, rather than just giving them a generic answer or pushing my own agenda. When they feel heard and understood, they're more likely to open up and trust me with their needs. It's not about me talking the most; it's about showing them that I care enough to listen. This simple shift in approach has made all the difference in building strong, lasting relationships with my clients.

For example, I had a seller who wanted to sell their home quickly but was fixated on a high asking price. Instead of immediately jumping in to explain why their price was too high for the market, I listened carefully to their reasons. They shared that they had made many memories in the house and were emotionally attached to it, which made it harder to let go. I acknowledged their feelings, saying, 'I can see how much this home means to you, and I understand why you feel it's worth more'.

By showing empathy and listening to their concerns, I was able to have a more productive conversation about the market realities. I then explained how pricing the home competitively could attract more buyers and lead to a quicker sale, which ultimately aligned with their goal of selling fast. This approach helped them feel heard and respected, and in the end, we came to a price that worked for both of us.

Listening wasn't just about gathering information – it was about understanding their needs and emotions, which allowed me to guide them to a decision they felt confident about. That's the power of listening, and it's been key in my success.

The SHV Formula: How to Build Likeability and Influence People to Like You

We all know people who seem to have an endless magnetic pull. They get seen, their ideas are heard, and they have a way of making others feel like they matter. These are the people who inspire others to act, work hard, and buy what they're selling. Wouldn't it be great if your clients felt that way about you? If they felt so comfortable and connected with you that they trusted you to guide them through their journey – whether that's buying a house, selling one, or making an investment? I believe that's where success lies.

Now, you don't have to be born with charisma to make an impression. You can work on becoming someone people like and trust. It starts with simple things: smile more, show real interest in others, and, most importantly, put away your phone and give your full attention to the person you're speaking with. People want to talk to someone who's engaged and curious about their lives – not someone who drones on about negative stuff or only talks about themselves.

For me, there's a key formula that I live by in almost every interaction: **Seen + Heard + Valued.** This is what makes people feel good and, more importantly, what keeps them coming back. When you apply this, you create a connection that makes them remember you.

Here's how I use this approach in real life. If I'm at an event or out in the community, and I see someone standing alone, I make a point to walk over and engage. Let's say I meet someone at a local event:

> 'Hi, I'm Zed. I really like your jacket! Where did you get it?' (THEY'RE BEING SEEN.)
> 'Oh, I live in Brighton.' (THEY'RE BEING HEARD.)
> 'Oh, I love Brighton! It's such a great spot. What do you like most about living here?' (THEY'RE BEING VALUED and they get to talk about what makes them happy or proud.)

Suddenly, that interaction becomes more than just a quick greeting. It's a real conversation. I've shown that I noticed them, took an interest in their life, and acknowledged something personal about them. People remember these because you're treating them like more than just a face in the crowd.

People love to feel remembered and appreciated.

If you take the time to engage with them, show genuine interest, and follow up, those relationships can turn into leads, clients, and even friends.

For me, building my business and network isn't about cold calling or just handing out business cards. It's about making real connections with people, where they feel seen, heard, and valued. After all, this is how you turn simple conversations into lasting relationships – and ultimately, into more opportunities for business. Keep that formula in mind, and you'll build your influence one genuine connection at a time.

12 KEY PRINCIPLES FOR BUILDING A STRONG REAL ESTATE CAREER AND LIFE

1. **The Past Cannot Be Changed.** No matter how much you dwell on it, the past is behind you. What matters most is how you move forward from here. Focus on the present and the future you want to create.
2. **Opinions Don't Define Your Reality.** Other people's views of you are just that – opinions. They don't define who you are or what you can achieve. Trust yourself and your abilities.
3. **Everyone's Journey is Different.** Don't compare your progress to someone else's. Each person has their own path, filled with unique challenges and victories. Embrace your own journey.
4. **Things Get Better With Time.** No matter how difficult things may seem now, time has a way of healing wounds and changing circumstances. Stay patient and keep moving forward.
5. **What Goes Around Comes Around.** The energy and actions you put into the world often come back to you. Treat others with kindness and respect, and you'll find it returns to you in unexpected ways.
6. **Stop Judging.** Everyone is fighting their own battles. Take a step back before passing judgment and offer understanding instead.

7. **Happiness is Found Within.** True happiness doesn't come from external sources – it's found within yourself. Cultivate a positive mindset, and your internal peace will radiate outward.
8. **Kindness is Free.** A kind word, a small gesture, or an understanding ear costs nothing but can mean everything. Don't underestimate the power of kindness.
9. **Smiles are contagious.** A smile can brighten someone's day, and it often has a ripple effect. When you smile, you invite positivity into the world around you.
10. **You Fail Only if You Quit.** Failure is part of the journey, not the end of it. You only fail when you give up. Keep going, and you will learn, grow, and eventually succeed.
11. **Positive Thoughts Create Positive Things.** Your mindset shapes your reality. Think positively, and you'll attract positive outcomes. Focus on the good, and the good will multiply.
12. **Energy You Put Out is The Energy You Will Receive.** The way you interact with the world and the energy you bring to every situation is often reflected back to you. Be intentional with the energy you share, and you'll invite similar energy into your life.

ZOLD!

MY FINAL WORDS

Throughout this book, I have aimed to pass on my experiences and learnings. Concepts and practices that have brought me huge success in selling real estate.

These aren't secrets. I want you to be successful, too. That's the reason behind my book.

I hope that you've been able to recognise the key factors that have contributed to me living beyond my wildest dreams and I also hope that these same factors will propel you to your best life.

But in true Z. Style, I will recap, just in case you're one of those readers who flip straight to the end of a book!

Know Your Product

Remember that when people look for a real estate agent, they want someone who knows the market well. They want to know how busy the market is, how many homes are Zelling. Therefore, know your area, your product, like the back of your hand. Knowledge gives you confidence.

Build A Team

Hire people who have the right attitude. You can train them in your specific industry. But if they have a positive attitude and are good with people, you know they'll fit in your team well.

Working with people also includes those who might not be members of your team, but are also valuable assets, a secret team who can help you. These brilliant people include librarians, receptionists, journalists, accountants, writers, bookkeepers and more. Leverage their resources, build relationships with them, and remember it's not a one-way street. You need to give something to them.

Believe in Yourself

Your customers don't just buy the product, they buy into YOU at first. Therefore, you need to embody self-confidence. Believe you are the best in the industry, and it will come.

Brand Yourself

You are your own brand. Everything must align – your presentation, your clothing, your physical and mental health.

Network, Network, Network

Every person you meet is a potential prospect. Be kind, be genuine, and keep their details. You never know when meeting someone will turn into a zale.

And finally ...

Before I started Z. Real Estate, I was just a dedicated agent in the busy world of real estate. Every day, I woke up with passion and a clear vision. I knew that success wasn't only about listings and sales; it was about being strong and resilient.

I often thought about an important truth: I can only win when my mind is stronger than my emotions. When faced with challenges – like a tough market or a difficult client – I learned to rely on discipline, which could solve 80percent of my problems. Each morning, I followed a routine that helped me focus and stay strong.

Believing in myself became a full-time job. There were no days off in this journey; it was a year-round commitment to growth and improvement. Each day brought new opportunities to push my limits, connect with clients, and build my reputation as a trusted adviser.

I kept a mantra in my mind: 'It's going to happen because I'm going to make it happen'. This belief drove my actions and reminded me that the power to succeed was within me. I knew that the road to success wasn't straight; it had ups and downs, doubts, and victories.

Some days felt heavy, and I thought about giving up. But I realised that both quitting and pushing through would come with their own pain. I chose to embrace the discomfort of growth instead of staying stuck.

With every challenge I faced, I grew stronger, not just as an agent but as a person. I became an inspiration for others in the real estate community, showing that success comes from discipline, belief, and the courage to keep going, no matter the obstacles. Looking back, I knew that every step I took brought me closer to where I wanted to be, leading me to create Z. Real Estate.

In the end, I didn't just reach my goals; I turned my journey into a story of resilience and triumph. I proved that with a strong mind and a disciplined heart, anything is possible.

And the same can be true for you.

Go reach for your dreams.

ACKNOWLEDGEMENTS

I want to start by acknowledging my father and my mother. Their unwavering support, guidance, and prayers have been the foundation of everything I've achieved. The values they instilled in me – the importance of hard work, integrity, and staying true to yourself – are the driving forces behind who I am today. Their blessings have been my power, their belief in me has been my fuel, and their love has been my anchor through every challenge.

To my amazing brothers, I am grateful every day to share this journey with you. Working alongside you has been one of the greatest privileges of my life. Your dedication, loyalty, and energy push me to be better, and I couldn't ask for a stronger team by my side.

To my incredible team at Z. Real Estate – you are the engine that makes everything possible. Your hard work, commitment, and belief in our vision allow me to dream bigger, push harder, and serve our clients at the highest level. I see the passion you bring every single day, and I'm proud to stand with you.

Every success, every lesson, every milestone is not just mine – it's ours. I'm blessed beyond measure to have my family and my team walking this path with me, and this book is as much a tribute to them as it is to my journey.

ENDNOTES

1 David Correll, *Social Media Statistics Australia November 2025*, in Social Media News Australia, https://www.socialmedianews.com.au/ 1 December 2025

2 Visual Marketing Australia, *Social Media Management,* accessed 13 April 2026, https://www.visualmarketing.com.au/social-media-management/

3 Naveen Kumar, *Facebook Users Statistics (2026) – Global Growth and Data Trends*, in DemandSage, https://www.demandsage.com/, accessed 25 February 2026

4 Bill Nash, *YouTube Shopping Statistics 2025*, in Marketing LTB, https://marketingltb.com/, 13 October 2025

5 Naveen Kumar, *Average Time Spent on Social Media per Day*, in DemandSage, https://www.demandsage.com/, 6 March 2026

6 2017, Murphy, Terri, "Scripts: New Ways to Handle Old Objections", RIS Media webinar, accessed 13 April 2026, https://www.rismedia.com/2017/10/26/scripts-new-ways-to-handle-old-objections/

7 Population: Census 2021, https://www.abs.gov.au/, 28 June 2022

8 Workplace Happiness Index 2025 Report, Seek, https://talent.seek.com.au/, 30 June 2025

NOTES

www.ingramcontent.com/pod-product-compliance
Lightning Source LLC
LaVergne TN
LVHW100335170926
848142LV00028B/118
* 9 7 8 1 7 6 4 5 6 1 9 1 4 *